STUDENT SELF-STUDY WORKBOOK

SHOW WHAT YOU KNOW® ON THE 8TH GRADE

FCAT

FLORIDA COMPREHENSIVE ASSESSMENT TEST

SCIENCE

grade

8

TEST-PREPARATION FOR THE FLORIDA COMPREHENSIVE ASSESSMENT TEST

Published by:

Show What You Know® Publishing
A Division of Englefield & Associates, Inc.
P.O. Box 341348
Columbus, OH 43234-1348
Phone: 1-877-PASSING (727-7464)
www.showwhatyouknowpublishing.com
www.passthefcat.com

FCAT Item Distribution information was obtained from the Florida Department of Education Website, April 2006.

Printed in the United States of America
08 07 06   20 19 18 17 16 15 14 13 12 11 10 9 8 7 6 5 4 3 2 1

ISBN: 1-59230-177-0

Acknowledgements

Show What You Know® Publishing acknowledges the following for their efforts in making this assessment material available for Florida students, parents, and teachers.

Cindi Englefield, President/Publisher
Eloise Boehm-Sasala, Vice President/Managing Editor
Christine Filippetti, Production Editor
Jill Borish, Production Editor
Charles V. Jackson, Project Editor
Jennifer Harney, Illustrator/Cover Designer

About the Contributors

The content of this book was written BY teachers FOR teachers and students and was designed specifically for the Florida Comprehensive Assessment Test (FCAT) for Grade 8. Contributions to the Science section of this book were also made by the educational publishing staff at Show What You Know® Publishing. Dr. Jolie S. Brams, a clinical child and family psychologist, is the contributing author of the Test Anxiety and Test-Taking Strategies chapters of this book. Without the contributions of these people, this book would not be possible.

Table of Contents

Introduction

Dear Student:

This *Show What You Know® on the FCAT for Grade 8 Science, Student Self-Study Workbook* was created to give you practice in preparation for the Florida Comprehensive Assessment Test (FCAT) in Science.

The first two chapters in this workbook—Test Anxiety and Test-Taking Strategies—were written especially for eighth-grade students. Test Anxiety offers advice on how to overcome nervous feelings you may have about tests. The Test-Taking Strategies chapter includes helpful tips on how to answer questions correctly so you can succeed on the Science section of the FCAT.

In the Science chapter of this book, you will find the following:

- A Science Glossary, a Science Reference Sheet, and a Periodic Table of the Elements are provided to review science terms.
- Scoring Guides for multiple-choice, gridded-response, short-response, and extended-response questions.
- You will answer multiple-choice, gridded-response, short-response, or extended-response questions on the Science Assessment. A Student Strategy is available for each benchmark to explain how to answer that benchmark's question correctly. An analysis for each tutorial question is also given to help you identify the correct answer.
- Two full-length Science Assessments follow the tutorial section for additional Science practice. An Answer Key will help you check to see if you answered the assessment questions correctly.

This Student Self-Study Workbook also includes a Science Assessment Correlation Chart. This chart can be used to identify individual areas of needed improvement.

This book will help you become familiar with the look and feel of the FCAT Science Assessment and will provide you with a chance to practice your test-taking skills to show what you know.

Good luck on the FCAT!

 © Englefield & Associates, Inc.

Test Anxiety

What Is Test Anxiety?

Test anxiety is a fancy term for feelings of worry and uneasiness that students feel before or during a test. Almost everyone experiences some anxiety at one time or another. Experiencing feelings of anxiety before any challenge is a normal part of life. However, when worrying about tests becomes so intense it interferes with test taking, or if worrying causes students mental or physical distress, this is called test anxiety.

What Are the Signs of Test Anxiety?

Test anxiety is much more than feeling nervous. In fact, students will notice test anxiety in four different areas: thoughts, feelings, behaviors, and physical symptoms. No wonder test anxiety gets in the way of students doing or feeling well.

Thoughts

Students with test anxiety usually feel overwhelmed with negative thoughts about tests and about themselves. These thoughts interfere with the ability to study and to take tests. Usually, these bothersome thoughts fall into three categories:

- *Worrying about performance*—A student who worries may have thoughts such as, "I don't know anything. What's the matter with me? I should have studied more. My mind is blank; now I'll never get the answer. I can't remember a thing; this always happens to me. I knew this stuff yesterday and now I can't do anything."

- *Comparing oneself to others*—A student who compares performance might say, "I know everyone does better than I do. I'm going to be the last one to finish this. Why does everything come easier for everyone else? I don't know why I have to be different than others."

- *Thinking about possible negative consequences* — A student with negative thoughts would think, "If I don't do well on this test, my classmates will make fun of me. If I don't do well on the FCAT Science test, my guidance counselor will think less of me. I won't be able to go to my favorite college. My parents are going to be angry."

Many of us worry or have negative thoughts from time to time. However, students with test anxiety have no escape and feel this worry whenever they study or take tests.

Feelings

In addition to having negative thoughts, students with test anxiety are buried by negative feelings. Students with test anxiety often feel:

- *Nervous and anxious* — Students feel jittery or jumpy. Anxious feelings may not only disrupt test taking but may interfere with a student's life in other ways. Small obstacles, such as misplacing a book, forgetting an assignment, or having a mild disagreement with a friend, may easily upset students. They may become preoccupied with fear, may have poor self-esteem, and may feel that the weight of the world is on their shoulders. They seem to be waiting for "the next bad thing to happen."

- *Confused and unfocused* — Students with test anxiety have their minds in hundreds of anxious places. They find it difficult to focus on their work, which makes studying for tests even harder. Students with test anxiety also have difficulty concentrating in other areas. When they should be listening in class, their minds worry about poor grades and test scores. They jump to conclusions about the difficulty of an upcoming test. They find themselves fidgeting. They constantly interrupt themselves while studying, or they forget how to complete simple assignments. Anxiety can interfere with a student's ability to focus, study, and learn.

- *Angry and resentful* — Test anxiety can lead to irritable and angry feelings. Anxious students are defensive when communicating with others. They become overwhelmed by negative thoughts and feel they are not good enough. Test anxiety also makes students feel "trapped" and as though they have no escape from school or tests. Students who feel there is no way out may get angry; they may resent the situation. They feel jealous of people they believe find school easier. They are angry at the demands placed on them. The more angry and resentful students become, the more isolated and alone they feel. This only leads to further anxiety and increased difficulties in their lives.

- *Depressed*—Anxiety and stress can lead to depression. Depression sometimes comes from "learned helplessness." When people feel they can never reach a goal and that they are never good enough to do anything, they tend to give up. Students who are overly anxious may get depressed. They lose interest in activities because they feel preoccupied with their worries about tests and school. It might seem as though they have no time or energy for anything. Some students with test anxiety give up on themselves completely, believing if they cannot do well in school (even though this may not be true), then why bother with anything?

Not all students with test anxiety have these feelings. If you or anyone you know seem to be overwhelmed by school, feel negative most of the time, or feel hopeless about school work (test taking included), you should look to a responsible adult for some guidance.

Behavior

Students with test anxiety often engage in behavior that gets in the way of doing well. When students have negative thoughts and feelings about tests, they participate in counterproductive behavior. In other words, they do things that are the opposite of helpful. Some students avoid tests altogether. Other students give up. Other students become rude and sarcastic, making fun of school, tests, and anything to do with learning. This is their way of saying, "We don't care." The truth is, they feel anxious and frustrated. Their negative behaviors are the result of thoughts and feelings that get in the way of their studying and test taking.

Physical Symptoms

All types of anxiety, especially test anxiety, can lead to very uncomfortable physical symptoms. Thoughts control the ways in which our bodies react, and this is certainly true when students are worried about test taking. Students with test anxiety may experience the following physical symptoms at one time or another:

- sweaty palms
- stomach pains
- "butterflies" in the stomach
- difficulty breathing
- feelings of dizziness or nausea
- headaches
- dry mouth
- difficulty sleeping, especially before a test
- decrease or increase in appetite

Test anxiety causes real physical symptoms. These symptoms are not made up or only in your head. The mind and body work together when stressed, and students can develop uncomfortable physical problems when they are anxious, especially when facing a major challenge like the FCAT.

The Test Anxiety Cycle

Have you ever heard the statement "one thing leads to another"? Oftentimes, when we think of that statement, we imagine Event A causes Event B, which leads to Event C. For example, being rude to your younger brother leads to an argument, which leads to upset parents, which leads to some type of punishment, like grounding. Unfortunately, in life, especially regarding test anxiety, the situation is more complicated. Although one thing does lead to another, each part of the equation makes everything else worse, and the cycle just goes on and on.

Let's think back again to teasing your younger brother. You tease your younger brother and he gets upset. The two of you start arguing and your parents become involved. Eventually, you get grounded. Sounds simple? It might get more complicated. When you are grounded, you might become irritable and angry. This causes you to tease your little brother more. He tells your parents, and you are punished again. This makes you even angrier, and now you don't just tease your little brother, you hide his favorite toy. This really angers your parents who now do not let you go to a school activity. That upsets you so much you leave the house and create trouble for yourself. One thing feeds the next. Well, the same pattern happens in the test anxiety cycle. Look at the following diagram.

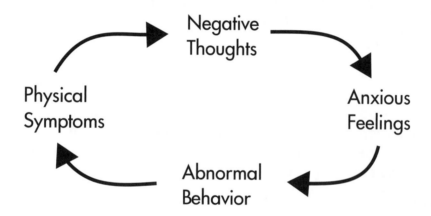

As you can see, the four parts of this diagram include the thoughts, feelings, behavior, and physical symptoms discussed earlier. When a student has test anxiety, each area makes the others worse. The cycle continues on and on. Here's an example:

Let's start off with some symptoms of negative thinking. Some students might say to themselves, "I'll never be able to pass the FCAT Science test!" This leads to feelings of frustration and anxiety. Because the student has these negative thoughts and feelings, his or her behavior changes. The student avoids tests and studying because they are nerve racking. Physical symptoms develop, such as the heart racing or the palms sweating. Negative thoughts then continue, "Look how terrible I feel; this is more proof I can't do well." The student becomes more irritable, even depressed. This affects behavioral symptoms again, making the student either more likely to avoid tests or perhaps not care about tests. The cycle goes on and on and on.

Is Test Anxiety Ever Good?

Believe it or not, a little worrying can go a long way! Too much test anxiety gets in the way of doing one's best, but students with no anxiety may also do poorly. Studies have shown that an average amount of anxiety can help people focus on tasks and challenges. This focus helps them use their skills when needed. Think about a sporting event. Whether a coach is preparing an individual ice skater for a competition or is preparing the football team for the Friday night game, getting each athlete "psyched up" can lead to a successful performance. A coach or trainer does not want to overwhelm the athlete. However, the coach wants to sharpen the senses and encourage energetic feelings and positive motivation. Some schools have a team dinner the night before a competition. This dinner provides some pleasant entertainment, but it also focuses everyone on the responsibilities they will have the next day.

Consider the graph below. You can see that too little test anxiety does not result in good test scores. As students become more concerned about tests, they tend to do better. But wait! What happens when too much anxiety is put into the equation? At that point, student performance decreases remarkably. When anxiety reaches a peak, students become frustrated and flustered. Their minds tend to blank out, they develop physical symptoms, they cannot focus, and they also behave in ways that interfere with their performance on tests.

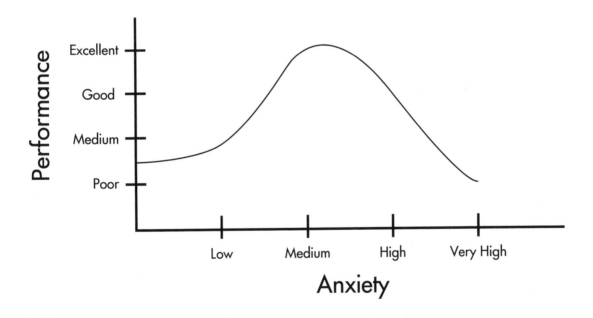

An important key to successful test taking is to get yourself in the right mood about taking a test. Looking at a test as a challenge and looking forward to meeting that challenge, regardless of the end result, is a positive and healthy attitude. You will feel excited, motivated, and maybe a little nervous but certainly ready to face the FCAT.

How Do I Tackle Test Anxiety?

Although test anxiety is an uncomfortable and frustrating feeling, the good news is you can win the battle over test anxiety. Conquering test anxiety will not be accomplished by luck or magic, but it can be done by students of all ages in a relatively short period of time. If you can learn to master test anxiety at this point in your life, you will be on the road to successfully facing many other challenges you will encounter.

Change the Way You Think

Whether you realize it or not, your thoughts—good and bad—influence your life. The way we think is related to how we feel about ourselves, how we get along with other people, and how well we do in school, especially when taking tests.

- *Positive Thinking Can Block Out Negative Thinking*—It is impossible to think two opposite thoughts at the same time. You may have one idea and then think about another, but one is always going to "win" over the other. When you practice positive thinking, you are replacing negative thoughts with positive ones. The more you are able to think positive thoughts, the less you will be troubled by negative ones.

- *The Soda Pop Test*—It's just as easy to have positive thoughts as negative ones. Everyone has heard the saying, "There is more than one side to any story." Just as there are two opinions on any given subject, there is generally more than one way to look at almost every situation in life. Some ways are more helpful than others.

Think about a can of soda pop. Draw a line down the middle of a blank piece of paper. On one side, put the heading, "All the bad things about this can of soda pop." On the other side, put another heading, "All the good things about this can of soda pop." Now, write appropriate descriptions or comments under each heading. For example, you could write, "This can of soda pop is a lot smaller than a two-liter bottle," which is negative thinking. Or, you could write, "This can of soda pop is just the right size to stay cold and fizzy until I finish it." It's easy to look at the soda-pop can and think bad thoughts. But you are also able to come up with many good things. If you spent all your time focusing on the negative aspects, you might believe the can of soda pop is bad. It is better to look at the positive side of things.

Part of successful test taking has to do with how you look at tests. With the can of soda pop, you could choose to think negatively, or you could have positive thoughts. The same holds true for tests. You can look at a test as a scary or miserable experience, or you can look at a test as just one of many challenges you will face in your life.

Counselors have known for years that people who are worried or anxious can become happier when thinking positive thoughts. Even when situations are scary, such as going to the dentist or having a medical test, "positive imagery" is very helpful. Positive imagery simply means focusing on good thoughts to replace anxious thoughts.

You can replace negative thoughts with positive ones through practice. Believe it or not, it really works!

- *Thoughts of Success*—Thinking "I can do it" thoughts chases away ideas of failure. Times that you were successful, such as when you did well in a sports event or figured out a complicated science question, are good things to think about. Telling yourself you have been successful in the past and can now master the Science section of the FCAT will replace thoughts that might otherwise cause anxiety.

- *Relaxing Thoughts*—Some people find that thinking calming or relaxing thoughts is helpful. Picturing a time in which you felt comfortable and happy can lessen your anxious feelings. Imagining a time when you visited the ocean, climbed a tree, or attended a concert can help you distract your mind from negative thoughts and focus on times that you were relaxed, happy, and felt positive.

- *All-or-Nothing Thinking*—Nothing is ever as simple as it seems. Sometimes we convince ourselves something is going to be awful or wonderful, but it rarely turns out that way.

No test is completely awful or completely perfect. Tests are going to have easy questions and hard questions, and you are going to have good test days and bad test days. The more you set up expectations that are all positive or negative, the more stressful the situation becomes. Accepting that nothing is totally good or bad, fun or boring, or easy or hard will reduce your anxiety and help you set reasonable expectations about tests. When you think about tests, try not to think about them as the road to academic success or a pit of failure. Instead, realize that all challenges have both good and bad elements, and you have to take everything in stride.

- *Making "Should" Statements*—Making "should" statements sets students up for failure. Sure, it is important to try your best, to study hard, and to make a reasonable effort on the FCAT; it may even be good to take an extra study session, try another practice test, or ask a teacher or tutor for advice and suggestions. It is also a good idea to use a book such as this one to help you do your best and show what you know. However, there is a big difference between doing your reasonable best and living your life with constant worries and put-downs. Students who constantly tell themselves "I should" and berate themselves for not having done everything possible only increase their levels of anxiety.

Go back to the test anxiety cycle. Suppose your thoughts are, "I should have stayed up an extra hour and studied," or "I should have reviewed those scientific formulas." The more you think these thoughts, the more anxious you get. The more anxious you get, the worse you feel. Again, the cycle goes on and on.

One part of maturing is learning to balance your life. Life is happiest when you find a good balance between being a lazy do-nothing and being a perfectionist. While we all know laziness gets us nowhere, being a perfectionist may actually paralyze your future chances of success because you will eventually fear meeting any new challenges. Failure does not mean real failure; it just means being imperfect. Preventing perfectionism begins by saying "no" to unreasonable thoughts and "should" statements. "Should" statements place high demands on a student and only lead to frustration and feelings of failure, shame, and anxiety.

Students who always think about what they "should" do often exhaust themselves by doing too much and worrying excessively. Exhaustion is another factor that leads to poor test-taking results.

Breaking the "should" habit means replacing "should" statements with positive comments about what you have accomplished and what you hope to reasonably accomplish in the future. For example, instead of saying, "I shouldn't have gone to the football game," or "I should have stayed home and studied," say, "I studied for two hours before the football game, and then I had a good time. Two hours was plenty to study for a science quiz. I need to have time for friends as well as studying. I concentrated while studying, and I think I did a good job. Even if I don't get a perfect score on the science quiz, I know I will do pretty well, and I gave myself the opportunity to do my best."

Control Physical Symptoms

Changing your physical response to stress can help break the test anxiety cycle. Relaxing is difficult when facing a major challenge such as the FCAT, but there are many proven techniques that can help you calm down.

- *Relax the Morning of the Test*—Try to allow yourself to relax the morning of the test. Engaging in some mild exercise, such as taking a walk, will relieve a lot of your physical stress. Some students may find that a workout the night before an exam makes them feel more relaxed and helps them sleep well. This is probably because the exercise distracts the student from the upcoming test. Also, intense exercise releases chemicals in the brain that cause you to feel calmer and happier. It may only take a quick walk around the block to help you relax and get your mind off your problems.

- *Listen to Music*—Listening to music in the morning before a test may also be helpful for students. It probably doesn't matter what kind of music you listen to as long as it makes you feel good about yourself, confident, and relaxed.

- *Relaxation Exercises*—Relaxation exercises are helpful to many students. Stress causes many physical changes in the body, including tenseness in all muscle groups, increased heart rate, and other physical symptoms. Learning simple exercises to feel less tense can also help break the test anxiety cycle.

Most exercises include tightening and releasing tension in your body as well as deep breathing. The purpose of all of these exercises is to distract you from the anxiety of an upcoming test and to allow your body to feel more loose and relaxed. These exercises can be completed while sitting at your desk, taking a test, or studying.

Try this simple relaxation exercise the next time you are tense. Sit upright in your chair, but allow yourself to be comfortable. Close your eyes and take four deep breaths in and out. When you get to the fourth breath, start breathing quietly but remain focused on your breathing. Start increasing the tension in your feet by squeezing your toes together tightly and then slowly releasing the pressure. Feel how relaxed your toes are feeling? Now tighten and release other muscle groups. Go from your legs to your stomach, to your shoulders, to your hands, and finally to your forehead. Squeeze and tighten your muscles and then relax them, all while focusing on your breathing. Once you practice this strategy, you might be able to feel more relaxed in a matter of seconds. This would be a good strategy to use during tests when you feel yourself becoming unfocused and anxious.

Prepare For the FCAT Science Assessment and Change the Way You Behave

Preparation always reduces anxiety. Taking the FCAT Science seriously, trying to do well on practice tests, and making an effort in all your classes will help you feel more confident and relaxed about the FCAT. Learning test-taking strategies can also give you a feeling of power and control over the test. No feeling is worse than realizing you are not prepared. Going into a test without ever having reviewed the FCAT Science material, looked at test-taking strategies, or concentrated on your schoolwork is very much like jumping out of an airplane without a parachute. You would be foolish if you were not panicked. Looking at the FCAT Science as just one more reason to take school seriously will help your grades, attitude, and success on the test.

Use Mental Preparation

Before the test, imagine in step-by-step detail how you will perform well and obtain a positive result. Several days before the test, think through the day of the test; repeat this as many times as you need. Imagine getting up in the morning, taking a nice shower, getting dressed in comfortable clothes, and listening to music on your way to school. Think about sitting in the testing room with a confident expression on your face. Imagine yourself remembering all of the strategies you read about in this book and learned in your classroom. Go through an imaginary test, step by step, practicing what you will do if you encounter a difficult question. You should also repeat the positive thoughts that should go through your head during the test. Preparation like this is key for reducing anxiety, as you already feel you have taken the test prior to ever having stepped in that testing room!

Don't Feel Alone

People feel more anxious when they feel alone and separate from others. Have you ever worried about a problem in your family or something going wrong at school? Things seem much worse when you are alone, but when you talk to someone who cares about you, you will find your problems soon seem less worrisome. Talk to your friends, parents, and teachers about your feelings. You will be surprised at the support you receive. Everyone has anxious feelings about tests. Having others understand your anxious feelings will help you accept yourself even more. Other people in your life can also give you suggestions about tests and can also help you put the FCAT Science and other tests in perspective.

Congratulate Yourself During the Test

Students with test anxiety spend a lot of time putting themselves down. They have never learned to say good things about themselves or to congratulate themselves on successes. As you go through the FCAT Science, try to find ways to mentally pat yourself on the back. If you find yourself successfully completing a difficult question, tell yourself you did a good job. When you finish reading a Science test item and feel you understand the information fairly well, remind yourself you are doing a good job in completing the FCAT Science. Paying attention to your successes, and not focusing on your failures, can greatly reduce test anxiety.

Test-Taking Strategies

Understand the Types of Questions on the Science Section of the FCAT

In preparing for the FCAT Science, you will need to think about the various types of questions you might be asked, but you also must think about and practice the different types of answers that will be required.

These types of answers require special approaches to thinking, and leave little room for random guessing. However, you will have the opportunity to use many of the science concepts that you have learned all through the eighth grade, as well as many of the skills you learned in other classes, such as Reading or Writing, where you were taught to write clearly and to the point. Some Science questions will also let you lean on other experiences you have had, or even your common sense.

Suppose you are asked questions about landfills and trash burning power plants. You may have forgotten the chemical symbols for sulphur dioxide or carbon monoxide, but you know about the impact of toxins in the food chain and a lot of other information from your biology class. You have also read the paper about a fight over a landfill in your own town. By carefully reading the information provided, considering the question, using all of your experiences, and being thankful to your teachers who taught you how to think and write, you can give an answer that makes sense.

Answer Every Question

In everyday life, it is rare for someone to have all of the answers all of the time, but an answer that is partially correct is much better than no answer at all! This is true for the FCAT Science. Even if you don't fully understand the material, or feel that you are running out of time, always try to answer the question. Incomplete answers that are sensible and accurate can receive partial credit. Most importantly, you can't lose points for trying!

Review all That You Have Learned Since Elementary School

The FCAT Science for Grade 8 contains questions that cover concepts and information that are taught not just in middle school, but throughout your schooling. If you are stressed about science, it might be helpful to take a look at some of your science textbooks from elementary school. Feeling comfortable with some basic definitions and concepts can go a long way toward doing your best. For example, review what you have learned about friction or gravity. Take another look at the concept of ecosystem. Help yourself remember basic chemical structures and the names of elements. Familiarize yourself with the structure of a cell.

A few minutes a day in review can lead to a big payoff on the FCAT Science for Grade 8.

Multiple-Choice Questions

Use "Codes" to Make Better Guesses

You might find it helpful to use codes to rate multiple-choice answers. Using your pencil in the test booklet, you can mark the following codes beside each of the four multiple-choice answers to see which is the best choice. An example of a code used by a eighth-grade student is given below.

(+) Put a plus sign by an answer choice if you are not sure if it is correct, but you think it might be correct;

(?) Put a question mark by an answer choice if you are not sure if it is the correct answer, but you don't want to rule it out completely;

(–) Put a minus sign by an answer choice if you are sure it is the wrong answer. (You then would choose from the other three choices to make an educated guess.)

Remember, it is fine to write in your test booklet. The space in the booklet is yours to use to help you do better on the FCAT. You will not have points counted off for using this coding system or creating your own system to help you on multiple-choice questions.

Answer Every Question

It is very important to answer as many multiple-choice questions as possible, even if you make an educated guess. On multiple-choice questions, you have a one in four chance of getting a question right, even if you just close your eyes and guess! This means for every four questions you guess, the odds are you will get about one (25%) of the answers right. Guessing alone is not going to make you a star on the FCAT, but leaving multiple-choice questions blank is not going to help you either.

Learn How to Power Guess

Not everything you know was learned in a classroom. Part of what you know comes from just living your day-to-day life. When you take the FCAT Science, you should use everything you have learned in school, but you should also use your experiences outside of the classroom to help you answer multiple-choice questions correctly. Using common sense, as well as your past experiences, will help you do especially well when answering multiple-choice items on the FCAT.

Now, take a look at this multiple-choice Science question:

> In her biology lab, Keisha was asked to observe and describe the cell wall of an onion plant cell. What materials or instruments would she need to complete this assignment?
>
> A. test tube, pipette, hot plate, saline solution
> B. iodine, electric scale, magnifying glass
> C. microscope, glass slide, methylene blue
> D. scalpel, dissecting pins, alcohol

To answer this question, you may not have to know all about onion cells, but you can use your general knowledge of science and your common sense to make a good guess. You can eliminate choices "A" and "D," because you know that you need something to help you see a very tiny cell, and there are no instruments in either of these choices that would be useful. Now the choice is between "B" and "C." Unfortunately, you can't remember having learned about methylene blue, but you figure that it must be a dye of some sort that would help make the cell more visible. You also know that while you have used a magnifying glass to help you identify the parts of leaves and flowers, it would not be strong enough to observe cells. Thus, "C" is a good guess and the correct answer!

Take Advantage of Chance

On the FCAT Science, multiple-choice questions carry less weight than short-response or extended-response items, but increasing your success on multiple-choice answers should increase your test taking-success. It is very important to answer as many multiple-choice questions as possible, even if you make a well thought-out guess, because luck is with you. If you can eliminate even one possible answer, your chances of success are even better. The best way to improve your chances on multiple-choice questions is to use strategies such as using codes and power guessing that are described in this chapter. Learning how to improve your chances by educated guessing is not cheating. In fact, you probably use this strategy outside of the classroom and don't even think about it. Imagine you have misplaced your favorite CD, and you want to find it before you leave for your friend's house. There are many possible places that it could be, but you use your common sense to eliminate some possibilities, thereby saving time searching and increasing your chances of finding it in time. For example, it might be possible that you left it in your sister's room, but you remember, "That isn't likely because her CD player has been broken for a month." That leaves you one less place to look, and more chances for success.

Gridded-Response Questions

How to Do Great with Those Grids

On the FCAT you will be asked to show some of your answers using grids. A grid gives you an organized way to show what you know. Once you take the time to learn about grids you will find them easy to use and helpful for test success. Using grids can seem tricky at first but no one is trying to trick you. All it takes is a little practice and some special hints and you can be the "gridmaster" of the universe!

Writing First, Bubbles Second

After you have figured out a numerical answer and checked your work (don't forget to always check your work), it is time to write your answer in the spaces at the top of the grid, called answer boxes. Fill in the written answer exactly as you will fill in the grid. For example, if the answer is 679, do not write the number using just any answer boxes. Remember, you will then fill in the answer bubble directly below your written answer, so if you are sloppy in writing your answer, it will be almost certain that you will fill in the bubbles incorrectly.

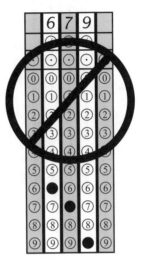

You will also see that some of the answer boxes and columns are shaded. This will help you easily see if the numbers in your answer are in the correct columns, or if you left an incorrect space blank. However, if you do not write your answers on the shaded areas dark enough to be read, you may end up filling in the wrong bubbles. Also be sure to fill in the bubbles with SOLID black marks that completely fill in the circle. Little dots, check marks, or incompletely filled bubbles will only lead to bubble trouble!

Right or Left, Left or Right, Either Way It Will Be All Right!

No matter what type of question, your answer will always fit into a five-column grid. You can choose to place the first digit of your answer in the left answer box column, or the last digit in the right answer box column. Some students feel more comfortable with one way or the other.

For example, let's say that the correct answer is 263. You could place the number 2 in the first column on the left side, or the 3 in the farthest right column. Both answers would be correct and would look like the grids below:

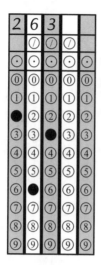 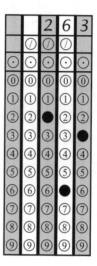

Be careful not to leave a blank answer box or column in the middle of an answer, although not all answers will use every space available.

Practice Makes Perfect

Many students think that filling in grids is no big deal but that type of thinking is not a good test-taking strategy. Once you begin to use grids, you will see that practice makes you more confident to show what you know by not wasting valuable test-taking time trying to remember how to fill in those grids. It can be frustrating to know the correct answer, but not know how to easily fill in the grids. So start with some simple problems and get comfortable filling in grids. It may sound silly, or even a little boring, but if filling in grids comes naturally, you can focus on finding the right answers instead of wondering if your answer will be scored correctly. Astronauts spend days learning how to use simple tools on a spacewalk, allowing them to concentrate on solving important problems. You may not be in space but your FCAT scores will soar if you practice filling in those grids!

Units? What Units?

Imagine that you are at home one day, the phone rings, and the caller says, "You are the grand prize winner of 100!" At first this sounds great! But then, wait…"A hundred of WHAT?" you ask yourself. A hundred dollars would be nice. A hundred feet of noodles may be less exciting. Paying attention to the units required in a gridded-response will help you on your way to test success. If the question asks for feet, then your answer needs to be in feet, not inches. While both answers may be correct, only the answer in feet will be scored as the correct answer.

What Are Those Slashes and Dots?

At first glance, the top part of a grid could look like some weird game of pool or checkers. Right under the gridded-response boxes are three bubbles with slashes and five bubbles with dots. The bubbles with slashes are used for showing fractions, and the bubbles with dots are used to show decimals.

Decimals are shown on grids just like you would show them on paper. But remember that decimals take up spaces just as numbers would. If your answer starts with a decimal, and you choose to put the first number of your answer in the farthest space to the left, that space will be a decimal (see the example farhest to the left). If you choose to put the last number of your answer in the farthest right space, the decimal may or may not be in the last space on the left, depending on the length of your answer and the appropriate placement of the decimal in your answer.

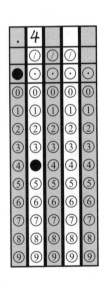

Fractions aren't hard to show either, provided that you do not write mixed numbers, such as $16\frac{1}{2}$, because this type of answer, although mathematically correct, cannot be scored using a grid. You must convert your answer to an improper fraction, such as $\frac{33}{2}$, or to a decimal such as 16.50. (This is a good reason to review the conversion of fractions.) The example below illustrates a correct answer using a mixed number.

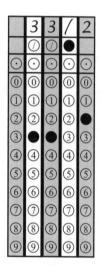
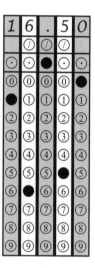

If asked, you can also express an answer in a percent. However, do not use decimals to show a percent. If you are trying to show 60%, or 60 percent, you could place your answer on the grid in these two ways:

When answering a gridded-response item remember to:

- Check your calculations
- Decide how to place your answer in the grid
- Carefully fill in the bubbles
- Make sure you use the correct units
- Double check to see that your answer is properly expressed in the grid

Short-Response Items

Write like a Scientist

Expressing ideas about science can be different than other types of writing. Science writing is specific. For example, when talking to your friends and describing your car troubles, you might say, "The more I drove, stuff just got louder and louder." The scientific way is to identify the subject of your comments and conclusions and to use correct terms of measurement and other vocabulary to be as precise and as clear as possible. A more scientific way of explaining your problem might be, "As the mileage increased on the car, the noise volume of the engine increased as well." Using "it" should also be avoided. For example, when describing the data on a graph, it is appropriate to write, "The temperature of the soil becomes warmer as the number of decomposers increase," instead of "It gets warmer as the number of decomposers increase." Tell the reader what "it" is.

Reviewing and using scientific vocabulary can also help you give the best possible answers on the FCAT Science.

Prepare Yourself for Various Short-Response Items

The good news is that short-response items on the FCAT Science for Grade 8 ask that you give short answers. Your answer could be:

> - a few words,
> - one or two sentences,
> - completing a chart or diagram,
> - making a brief comparison or contrast, or
> - writing a brief conclusion.

As you prepare for the FCAT, practice giving all of these answers. Try to become an active learner during regular class time and during any preparation for the FCAT. Imagine how you could answer different questions in different ways. You might want to try this in real life. Think of all the ways you could try to convince your parents to let you have a dog. While the brief statement, "I desperately want a dog!" may not work, you could provide a concise comparison or contrast, such as, "Research shows that students who have a dog are more pleasant and have better grades." This is well spoken, although not guaranteed to work.

Don't Let Your Handwriting Be Frightening

On short-response and extended-response items, you will be asked to write answers. Most students usually rely on computers to write assignments, and neat handwriting isn't always the first thing on their minds. Remember, even "science geniuses" will not do their best on the FCAT Science for grade 8 unless the scorer can read their answers. No matter how rushed you may feel, take your time with your handwriting. It doesn't have to win awards, but it has to be legible.

Carefully Look at The Required Response

In most instances, the type of response that is required will be made clear in the question. In order to not waste time, and to give the best possible answer, make sure to carefully understand how you are asked to respond. Sometimes the answer booklet will lay out the way to respond. For example, there may be a blocked space for a one word answer, and then a longer space for the definition. Ignoring what is in front of you is not a good idea.

Suppose you review a diagram describing the manner in which metabolic energy was created. The short-response question might be, "In the space below, write down the word that describes the unit of energy used to measure metabolism in humans. Then, write a sentence that explains a situation in which this measure is helpful." You should not leave the one word answer blank. You also know that you need to use one example to explain or define that measure. (The answer is "calorie," and it could be used by experts in sports physiology to determine what and when athletes eat before a competition.)

Extended-Response Items

Don't Avoid Extended-Response Items

Extended-response items can be intimidating for some students, especially if they feel that they are weaker in science than in other subjects. While there are fewer extended-response items on the FCAT, your answers are important in helping you do well on the FCAT Science .

Keep in mind that even a partially correct answer will increase your score, and there is no penalty for trying. If you find yourself feeling anxious about these more complex questions, review the section of this book about test anxiety, or talk to your science teacher or school counselor.

Don't Forget to Label

In both short-response and extended-response items, you might be asked to create a diagram, graph, or picture to explain your answer. Although you might know what you mean, the reader cannot read your mind. Make sure that you label or identify each axis of a graph, the columns of a table, or the objects in a picture. Not only will this help the reader of your test, but as you label your work, you will have a chance to review your thinking and make sure that your conclusions make sense.

To Do Your Best on Extended-Response Items, Practice Short-Response Items First

Like short-response questions, extended-response questions require thinking and ask the student to respond in a variety of possible ways. Many students find it more effective to feel comfortable with short-answer questions first and then to move on to tackling extended-response questions.

Detailed Answers Rule

It is hard to show what you know if you don't include details. Suppose you are asked to compare two experiments to determine which type of battery is best in wet conditions. One experiment tested three different battery types when submerged in a tub of water, and the other experiment tested the same battery types when soaked with a damp cloth. Stating, "The environments were not the same, so the experiments cannot be adequately compared," may be generally correct, but further explaining that water pressure is also a variable provides the type of detail that lets the reader of your answer understand your reasoning and mastery of science.

Use Your Pencil to Your Advantage

Don't hesitate to make an outline of your answer on the margins of your test booklet. Look at extended-response items as you would an essay question and take some time to write down the structure of your response. Then, add details. Thinking first and writing later is always a good idea.

Be The Teacher for The Day

Extended-response answers require you to be the teacher. Extended responses often ask that you explain your answer in a way that is complete and understandable. Ask yourself, "If I were explaining my answer to friends, would they understand?" Express your answers in a step-by-step manner, explaining your reasoning as you proceed. Don't assume that your "student" knows everything or can read your mind.

Know Your Tools

On the FCAT Science, you may use a calculator to find answers. These questions test your ability to understand the process of finding a correct answer, not your skills at quickly performing routine calculations without help. Unfortunately, using a calculator won't be helpful if you don't know how to quickly and accurately use a calculator, and may actually cause you to arrive at the wrong answer.

Using a calculator takes practice. When you first learned a computer keyboard, you probably were slower and made many more mistakes. If you rely on your parents or friends to type for you, you probably haven't improved your keyboarding skills very much since elementary school. If you had to type your answers on the FCAT, it would take you a long time, and you would have many mistakes. The same amount of practice is needed for a calculator in order for it to be helpful to you on the FCAT Science. Students who avoid using a calculator except when absolutely necessary will not benefit from using one when taking the FCAT. So, if you are not comfortable with a calculator, practice! It will not only help you on the test, but you will find this skill valuable in jobs and for solving problems in your everyday life.

Science

Introduction

In the Science section of the Florida Comprehensive Assessment Test (FCAT), you will be asked questions designed to assess the knowledge you have gained throughout your academic career. These questions have been constructed based on the science skills you have been taught in school through the eighth grade. Within this section of the FCAT, your knowledge will be assessed with multiple-choice, gridded-response, short-response, and extended-response items. The questions are not meant to confuse you or to trick you, but are written so you have the best opportunity to show what you know about Science.

This *Show What You Know® on the FCAT Science for Grade 8, Student Self-Study Workbook* contains the following:

- The Sunshine State Standards (Strands, Standard, and Benchmarks)
- The Science Practice Tutorial with a sample question for each benchmark tested, sample responses, and an answer key with in-depth analyses.
- Two full-length Science Assessments with sample responses, correlation charts, and answer keys with in-depth analyses.

Show What You Know® on the FCAT Science for Grade 8, Student Self-Study Workbook will help you practice your test-taking skills. The Science Practice Tutorial and two full-length Science Assessments have been created to model the Grade 8 Florida Comprehensive Assessment Test in Science.

Understanding Grade Level Expectations

Subject Area: SC: Science

A **strand** is a category of knowledge. The eight strands assessed on the FCAT Science test are The Nature of Matter, Energy, Force and Motion, Processes That Shape The Earth, Earth and Space, Processes of Life, How Living Things Interact With Their Environment, and The Nature of Science

Each Science **standard** is a general statement of expected student achievement within a strand. The standards are the same for all grade levels.

Benchmarks are specific statements of expected student achievement under each Science standard. Test items are written to assess the benchmarks. In some cases, two or more related benchmarks are grouped together because the assessment of one benchmark necessarily addresses another benchmark.

SC: Science

Strand A: The Nature of Matter

Standard 1:
The student understands that all matter has observable measurable properties.

1. Identifies various ways in which substances differ (e.g., mass, volume, shape, density, texture, and reaction to temperature and light). [Also assesses: SC.A.1.3.2 understands the difference between weight and mass. SC.A.1.3.6 knows that equal valumes of different substances may have different masses.]

The Grade Level Expectation's **Numbering System** identifies the Subject Area, the Strand, the Level, and the Benchmark. For example, in the Grade Level Expectation (SC.A.1.3.1), the first letters (SC) stand for the Subject Area, Science, and the second letter (A.) for the Strand, (The Nature of Matter). The first number (1.) stands for the Standard, the second number (3.) for the Level (Grades 6–8), the third number (1.) for the Benchmark. **Note:** The Grade Level Expectations are not intended to take the place of a curriculum guide, but rather to serve as the basis for curriculum development to ensure that the curriculum is rich in content and is delivered through effective instructional activities. The Grade Level Expectations are in no way intended to limit learning, but rather to ensure that all students across the state receive a good educational foundation that will prepare them for a productive life.

Sunshine State Standards

Science

Strand A: The Nature of Matter
Standard 1: The student understands that all matter has observable, measurable properties.

SC.A.1.3.1 The student identifies various ways in which substances differ (e.g., mass, volume, shape, density, texture, and reaction to temperature and light). [Also assesses: SC.A.1.3.2 The student understands the difference between weight and mass. SC.A.1.3.6 The student knows that equal volumes of different substances may have different masses.]

SC.A.1.3.3 The student knows that temperature measures the average energy of motion of the particles that make up the substance.

SC.A.1.3.4 The student knows that atoms in solids are close together and do not move around easily; in liquids, atoms tend to move farther apart; in gas, atoms are quite far apart and move around freely.

SC.A.1.3.5 The student knows the difference between a physical change in a substance (i.e., altering the shape, form, volume, or density) and a chemical change (i.e., producing new substances with different characteristics).

Standard 2: The student understands the basic principles of atomic theory.

SC.A.2.3.1 The student describes and compares the properties of particles and waves.

SC.A.2.3.2 The student knows the general properties of the atom (a massive nucleus of neutral neutrons and positive protons surrounded by a cloud of negative electrons) and accepts that single atoms are not visible.

Strand B: Energy

Standard 1: The student recognizes that energy may be changed in form with varying efficiency.

SC.B.1.3.1 The student identifies forms of energy and explains that they can be measured and compared. [Also assesses: A.2.3.3 The student knows that radiation, light, and heat are forms of energy used to cook food, treat diseases, and provide energy. B.1.3.2 The student knows that energy cannot be created or destroyed, but only changed from one form to another. SC.B.1.3.3 The students knows that various forms in which energy comes to Earth from the sun (e.g., visible light, infrared, and microwave).]

SC.B.1.3.4 The student knows that energy conversions are never 100% efficient (i.e., some energy is transformed to heat and is unavailable for further useful work).

SC.B.1.3.5 The student knows the processes by which thermal energy tends to flow from a system of higher temperature to a system of lower temperature.

SC.B.1.3.6 The student knows the properties of waves (e.g., frequency, wavelength, and amplitude); that each wave consists of a number of crests and troughs; and the effects of different media on waves. [Also assesses: SC.C.1.3.2 The student knows that vibrations in materials set up wave disturbances that spread away from the source (e.g., sound and earthquake waves).]

Standard 2: The student understands the interaction of matter and energy.

SC.B.2.3.1 The student knows that most events in the universe (e.g., weather changes, moving cars, and the transfer of a nervous impulse in the human body) involve some form of energy transfer and that these changes almost always increase the total disorder of the system and its surroundings, reducing the amount of useful energy.

Strand C: Force and Motion

Standard 1: The student understands that types of motion may be described, measured, and predicted.

SC.C.1.3.1 The student knows that the motion of an object can be described by its position, direction of motion, and speed.

Standard 2: The student understands that the types of force that act on an object and the effect of that force can be described, measured, and predicted.

SC.C.2.3.1 The student knows that many forces (e.g., gravitational, electrical, and magnetic) act at a distance (i.e., without contact).

SC.C.2.3.4 The student knows that simple machines can be used to change the direction or size of a force.

SC.C.2.3.6 The student explains and shows the ways in which a net force (i.e., the sum of all acting forces) can act on an object (e.g., speeding up an object traveling in the same direction as the net force, slowing down an object traveling in the direction opposite of the net force). [Also assesses: SC.C.2.3.2 The student knows common contact forces. SC.C.2.3.3 The student knows that if more than one force acts on an object, then the forces can reinforce or cancel each other, depending on their direction and magnitude. SC.C.2.3.5 The student understands that an object in motion will continue at a constant speed and in a straight line until acted upon by a force and that an object at rest will remain at rest until acted upon by a force.]

SC.C.2.3.7 The student knows that gravity is a universal force that every mass exerts on every other mass.

Strand D: Processes that Shape the Earth
Standard 1: The student recognizes that processes in the lithosphere, atmosphere, hydrosphere, and biosphere interact to shape the Earth.

SC.D.1.3.1 The student knows that mechanical and chemical activities shape and reshape the Earth's land surface by eroding rock and soil in some areas and depositing them in other areas, sometimes in seasonal layers.

SC.D.1.3.3 The student knows how conditions that exist in one system influence the conditions that exist in other systems.

SC.D.1.3.4 The student knows the ways in which plants and animals reshape the landscape (e.g., bacteria, fungi, worms, rodents, and other organisms add organic matter to the soil, increasing soil fertility, encouraging plant growth, and strengthening resistance to erosion). [Also assesses: SC.D.1.3.2 The student knows that over the whole earth, organisms are growing, dying, and decaying as new organisms are produced by the old ones.]

SC.D.1.3.5 The student understands concepts of time and size relating to the interaction of Earth's processes (e.g., lightning striking in a split second as opposed to the shifting of the Earth's plates altering the landscape, distance between atoms measured in Angstrom units as opposed to distance between stars measured in light-years).

Strand E: Earth and Space
Standard 1: The student understands the interaction and organization in the Solar System and the universe and how this affects life on Earth.

SC.E.1.3.1 The student understands the vast size of our Solar System and the relationship of the planets and their satellites. [Also assesses: SC.E.1.3.2 The student knows that available data from various satellite probes show the similarities and differences among planets and their moons in the Solar System.]

SC.E.1.3.4 The student knows that stars appear to be made of similar chemical elements, although they differ in age, size, temperature, and distance.

Standard 2: The student recognizes the vastness of the universe and the Earth's place in it.

SC.E.2.3.1 The student knows that thousands of other galaxies appear to have the same elements, forces, and forms of energy found in our Solar System. [Also assesses: SC.E.1.3.3 The student understands that our sun is one of many stars in our galaxy.]

Strand F: Processes of Life
   Standard 1: The student describes patterns of structure and function in living things.

SC.F.1.3.1 The student understands that living things are composed of major systems that function in reproduction, growth, maintenance, and regulation.

SC.F.1.3.2 The student knows that the structural basis of most organisms is the cell and most organisms are single cells, while some, including humans, are multicellular.

SC.F.1.3.3 The student knows that in multicellular organisms cells grow and divide to make more cells in order to form and repair various organs and tissues.

SC.F.1.3.4 The student knows that the levels of structural organization for function in living things include cells, tissues, organs, systems, and organisms.

SC.F.1.3.5 The student explains how the life functions of organisms are related to what occurs within the cell.

SC.F.1.3.6 The student knows that the cells with similar functions have similar structures, whereas those with different structures have different functions.

SC.F.1.3.7 The student knows that behavior is a response to the environment and influences growth, development, maintenance, and reproduction.

Standard 2: The student understands the process and importance of genetic diversity.

SC.F.2.3.1 The student knows the patterns and advantages of sexual and asexual reproduction in plants and animals.

SC.F.2.3.2 The student knows that the variation in each species is due to the exchange and interaction of genetic information as it is passed from parent to offspring.

SC.F.2.3.3 The student knows that generally organisms in a population live long enough to reproduce because they have survival characteristics.

SC.F.2.3.4 The student knows that the fossil record provides evidence that changes in the kinds of plants and animals in the environment have been occurring over time.

Strand G: How Living Things Interact with Their Environment
Standard 1: The student understands the competitive, interdependent, cyclic nature of living things in the environment.

SC.G.1.3.2 The student knows that biological adaptations include changes in structures, behaviors, or physiology that enhance reproductive success in a particular environment.

SC.G.1.3.3 The student understands that the classification of living things is based on a given set of criteria and is a tool for understanding biodiversity and interrelationships.

SC.G.1.3.4 The student knows that the interactions of organisms with each other and with the nonliving parts of their environments result in the flow of energy and the cycling of matter throughout the system. [Also assesses: SC.G.1.3.1 The student knows that viruses depend on other living things. SC.G.1.3.5 The student knows that life is maintained by a continuous input of energy from the sun and by the recycling of the atoms that make up the molecules of living organisms.]

Standard 2: The student understands the consequences of using limited natural resources.

SC.G.2.3.1 The student knows that some resources are renewable and others are nonrenewable. [Also assesses: SC.B.2.3.2 The student knows that most of the energy used today is derived from burning stored energy collected by organisms millions of years ago (i.e., nonrenewable fossil fuels).]

SC.G.2.3.2 The student knows that all biotic and abiotic factors are interrelated and that if one factor is changed or removed, it impacts the availability of other resources within the system.

SC.G.2.3.3 The student knows that a brief change in the limited resources of an ecosystem may alter the size of a population or the average size of individual organisms and that long-term change may result in the elimination of animal and plant populations inhabiting the Earth.

SC.G.2.3.4 The student understands that humans are a part of an ecosystem and their activities may deliberately or inadvertently alter the equilibrium in ecosystems. [Also assesses: SC.D.2.3.2 The student knows the positive and negative consequences of human action on the Earth's systems.]

Strand H: The Nature of Science
Standard 1: The student uses the scientific processes and habits of mind to solve problems.

SC.H.1.3.1 The student knows that scientific knowledge is subject to modification as new information challenges prevailing theories and as a new theory leads to looking at old observations in a new way.

SC.H.1.3.2 The student knows that the study of the events that led scientists to discoveries can provide information about the inquiry process and its effects.

SC.H.1.3.3 The student knows that science disciplines differ from one another in topic, techniques, and outcomes, but that they share a common purpose, philosophy, and enterprise.

SC.H.1.3.4 The student knows that accurate record keeping, openness, and replication are essential to maintaining an investigator's credibility with other scientists and society. [Also assesses: SC.H.1.3.7 The student knows that when similar investigations give different results, the scientific challenge is to verify whether the differences are significant by further study.]

SC.H.1.3.5 The student knows that a change in one or more variables may alter the outcome of an investigation.

Standard 2: The student understands that most natural events occur in comprehensible, consistent patterns.

SC.H.2.3.1 The student recognizes that patterns exist within and across systems.

SC.H.3.3.1 The student knows that science ethics demand that scientists must not knowingly subject coworkers, students, the neighborhood, or the community to health or property risks. [Also assesses: SC.H.3.3.2 The student knows that special care must be taken in using animals in scientific research. SC.H.3.3.3 The student knows that in research involving human subjects, the ethics of science require that potential subjects be fully informed about the risks and benefits associated with the research and of their right to refuse to participate.]

SC.H.3.3.4 The student knows that technological design should require taking into account constraints such as natural laws, the properties of the materials used, and economic, political, social, ethical, and aesthetic values. [Also assesses: SC.H.3.3.6 The student knows that no matter who does science and mathematics or invents things, or when or where they do it, the knowledge and technology that result can eventually become available to everyone. SC.H.3.3.37 The student knows that computers speed up and extend people's ability to collect, sort, and analyze data; prepare research reports; and share data and ideas with others.]

About the FCAT Science for Grade 8

Items in this section of the FCAT will test your ability to connect and apply science concepts and processes to everyday events. Eighth-grade students are also allowed to use the Science Reference Sheet and the Periodic Table during testing. Learning science actively will engage you in the world and should enable you to:

- engage in quantitative and qualitative observations;

- investigate thoughtful questions;

- make logical predictions;

- design and conduct experiments and other types of investigations;

- collect and organize data;

- offer reasonable explanations;

- explore possible conclusions;

- communicate their understanding; and

- make well-reasoned, data-based decisions and communicate them effectively.

The FCAT Science will ask you multiple-choice items, gridded-response items, short-response and extended-response tasks (Read, Inquire, Explain). For more in-depth information on how to answer these different types of questions please refer to pages 12–22 of this *Show What You Know® on the FCAT Science for Grade 8, Student Self-Study Workbook.*

For multiple-choice items, each question has only one correct answer; the other three choices are distractors representing incorrect answers that students commonly obtain for the question. Multiple-choice items are worth one point each. Students should spend no more than one minute answering each individual question, but they should be sure to allow themselves time to scrutinize each possible choice.

Gridded-response items also have only one correct answer, but in certain circumstances, the answer may be represented in different formats. For example, if a question asks what fraction is equal to 50%, students may respond with 1/2, 4/8, 50/100, or any other fraction equaling 50%. Gridded-response questions are worth one point each.

The "Think, Solve, and Explain" questions allow partial credit for some answers, even if they are not 100% correct. Answers will be scored and points will be given based on the completeness and correctness of the answers. If a portion of an answer is correct, a portion of the points will be awarded.

Rubric for Short-Response Questions

2 points A score of two indicates that the student has demonstrated a thorough understanding of the scientific concepts and/or procedures embodied in the task. The student has completed the task correctly, in a scientifically sound manner. When required, student explanations and/or interpretations are clear and complete. The response may contain minor flaws that do not detract from the demonstration of a thorough understanding.

1 point A score of one indicates that the student has provided a response that is only partially correct. For example, the student may arrive at an acceptable conclusion or provide an adequate interpretation, but may demonstrate some misunderstanding of the underlying scientific concepts and/or procedures. Conversely, a student may arrive at an unacceptable conclusion or provide a faulty interpretation, but could have applied appropriate and scientifically sound concepts and/or procedures.

0 points A score of zero indicates that the student has provided a response that demonstrates no understanding of the science embodied in the task. The student explanation may be incorrect, uninterpretable, or contain clear misunderstanding of the underlying scientific concepts and/or procedures.

Rubric for Extended-Response Questions

4 points   A score of four indicates that the student has demonstrated a thorough understanding of the scientific concepts and/or procedures embodied in the task. The student has completed the task correctly, used scientifically sound procedures, and provided clear and complete explanations and interpretations.

The response may contain minor flaws that do not detract from a demonstration of a thorough understanding.

3 points   A score of three indicates that the student has demonstrated an understanding of the scientific concepts and/or procedures embodied in the task. The student's response to the task is essentially correct, but the scientific procedures, explanations, and/or interpretations provided are not thorough.

The response may contain minor flaws that reflect inattentiveness or indicate some misunderstanding of the underlying scientific concepts and/or procedures.

2 points   A score of two indicates that the student has demonstrated only a partial understanding of the scientific concepts and/or procedures embodied in the task. Although the student may have arrived at an acceptable conclusion or provided an adequate interpretation of the task, the student's work lacks an essential understanding of the underlying scientific concepts and/or procedures.

The response may contain errors related to misunderstanding important aspects of the task, misuse of scientific procedures/processes, or faulty interpretations of results.

1 point   A score of one indicates that the student has demonstrated a very limited understanding of the scientific concepts and/or procedures embodied in the task. The student's response is incomplete and exhibits many flaws. Although the student's response has addressed some of the conditions of the task, the student has reached an inadequate conclusion and/or provided reasoning that is faulty or incomplete.

The response exhibits many flaws or may be incomplete.

0 points   A score of zero indicates that the student has provided a response that demonstrates no understanding of the science embodied in the task. The student explanation may be incorrect, uninterpretable, or contain clear misunderstanding of the underlying scientific concepts and/or procedures.

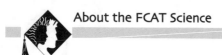
Using the Skills Charts

The Skills Charts on pages 199–200 and 246–247 show the correct answers for each Assessment Test question, the standards covered by each question, and some keywords that indicate the subject covered by each question. Students can use the chart as they score their tests to see which standards they may need to review before taking the FCAT Science Test.

Using the Correlation Charts

The Correlation Charts on pages 210–212 and 255–257 can be used by the teachers to identify areas of improvement. When students miss a question, place an "X" in the corresponding box. A column with a large number of "Xs" shows more practice is needed with that particular standard. Permission is granted by the publisher to reproduce the Correlation Charts to one teacher for use in a single classroom.

Grade 8 FCAT Science Reference Sheet

Equations

Acceleration ($\bar{a}$)	=	$\dfrac{\text{change in velocity (m/s)}}{\text{time taken for this change (s)}}$	$\bar{a} = \dfrac{v_f - v_i}{t_f - t_i}$

Average speed ($\bar{v}$)	=	$\dfrac{\text{distance}}{\text{time}}$	$\bar{v} = \dfrac{d}{t}$

Density (D)	=	$\dfrac{\text{mass (g)}}{\text{Volume (cm}^3\text{)}}$	$D = \dfrac{m}{V}$

Percent Efficiency (e)	=	$\dfrac{\text{Work out (J)}}{\text{Work in (J)}} \times 100$	$\%e = \dfrac{W_{out}}{W_{in}} \times 100$

Force in newtons (F)	=	mass (kg) x acceleration (m/s^2)	$F = ma$

Frequency in hertz (f)	=	$\dfrac{\text{number of events (waves)}}{\text{time (s)}}$	$f = \dfrac{n \text{ of events}}{t}$

Momentum (ρ)	=	mass (kg) x velocity (m/s)	$\rho = mv$

Wavelength (λ)	=	$\dfrac{\text{velocity (m/s)}}{\text{frequency (Hz)}}$	$\lambda = \dfrac{v}{f}$

Work (W)	=	Force (N) x distance (m)	$W = Fd$

Units of Measure

m = meter   g = gram   s = second
cm = centimeter   kg = kilogram   Hz = hertz (waves per second)
  J = joule (newton-meter)
  N = newton (kilogram-meter per second squared)

Periodic Table of Elements

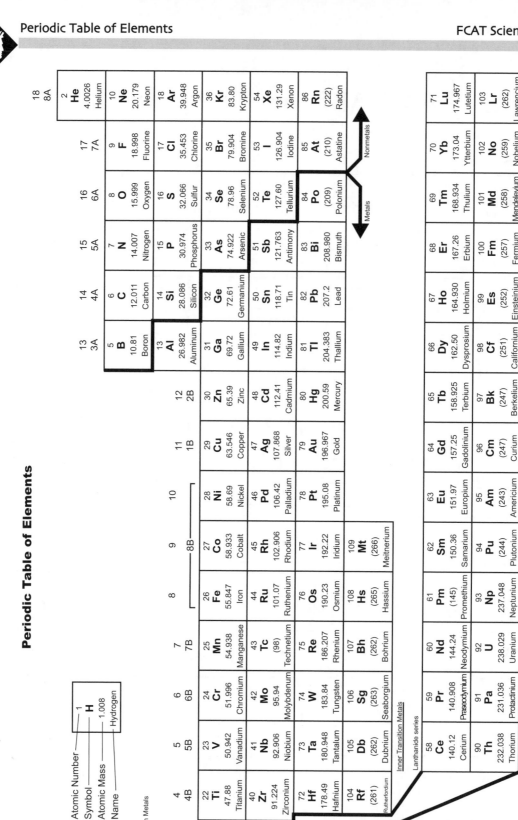

GLOSSARY

abiotic: An environmental factor not associated with the activities of living organisms.

acceleration: Rate of change in velocity, usually expressed in meters per second; involves an increase or decrease in speed and/or a change in direction.

accuracy: The ability to be precise and avoid errors.

acid: A compound, usually water-soluble, that releases hydrogen ions when in solution. An acid reacts with a base to form a salt, has a pH less than 7, and turns blue litmus red. Acids are corrosive and have a sour taste.

acidity: The concentration of an acid in a substance, often measured in terms of pH.

acquired (learned) characteristic: Modifications produced in an individual plant or animal as a result of mutilation, disease, use and disuse, or any distinctly environmental influence.

adaptation: The development of physical and behavioral characteristics that allow organisms to survive and reproduce in their habitats.

air pressure: The downward pressure exerted by the weight of the overlying atmosphere. It has a mean value of one atmosphere at sea level but decreases as elevation increases.

air resistance: Force of air on moving objects.

allele: Any of two or more alternate forms of a gene that an organism may have for a particular trait.

amplitude: In any periodic function (e.g., a wave) the maximum absolute variation of the function.

artery: A blood vessel that is part of the system carrying blood under pressure from the heart to the rest of the body.

asexual reproduction: A form of reproduction in which new individuals are formed without the involvement of gametes.

atmosphere: The mixture of gases that surrounds a celestial body such as Earth.

atom: The smallest portion into which an element can be divided and still retain its properties, made up of a dense, positively charged nucleus surrounded by a system of electrons.

attract: To draw objects nearer (for example, as a magnet draws iron objects toward itself).

axis: The imaginary line on which an object rotates (e.g., Earth's axis runs through Earth between the North Pole and the South Pole); an imaginary straight line that runs through a body; a reference to the line in a coordinate system or graph.

bacteria: Single-celled, often parasitic microorganisms without distinct nuclei or organized cell structures. Various species are responsible for decay, fermentation, nitrogen fixation, and many plant and animal diseases.

biodiversity: The existence of a wide range of different species in a given area or specific period of time.

biotic: Factors in an environment relating to, caused by, or produced by living organisms.

blood vessel: Any of the arteries, veins, or capillaries through which blood flows.

GLOSSARY

body of water: The part of Earth's surface covered with water, such as a river, lake, or ocean.

calorie: Unit of energy; the amount of heat needed to raise one gram of water one degree Celsius at standard atmospheric pressure.

camouflage: The devices that animals use to blend into their environment in order to avoid being seen by predators or prey, especially coloration.

carbohydrates: An organic compound derived from carbon, hydrogen, and oxygen that is an important source of food and energy for humans and animals. Sugar, starch, and cellulose are carbohydrates.

carbon dioxide: A heavy, colorless, odorless atmospheric gas produced during respiration and used by plants during photosynthesis. It is also formed by combustion, and increasing atmospheric levels may alter Earth's climate. Symbol: CO_2.

carnivore: An animal or plant that consumes or obtains nutrients from animals.

cell: The smallest unit of living matter capable of functioning independently.

change of state: A physical change that occurs when matter changes to another state (i.e., liquid, gas, or solid).

charge: A fundamental characteristic of matter, responsible for all electric and electromotive forces, expressed in two forms known as positive and negative.

chemical: A substance used in or produced by the processes of chemistry.

chemical weathering: The breakdown and alteration of rocks at or near Earth's surface as a result of chemical processes.

circuit: A route around which an electrical current can flow, beginning and ending at the same point.

cleavage of minerals: The splitting of minerals or rocks along natural planes of weakness.

cold-blooded: Used to describe an animal with an internal body temperature that varies according to the temperature of the surroundings.

community: All the populations of organisms belonging to different species and sharing the same geographical area.

compare: To examine two or more people or things in order to discover similarities and differences between them.

compound: Something made by the combination of two or more different things.

condensation: The process of changing from a gas (i.e. water vapor) to a liquid (i.e. dew); the act of making more dense or compact.

conservation: Controlled use and/or maintenance of natural resources; various efforts to preserve or protect natural resources.

conservation of energy: A fundamental principle stating energy cannot be created nor destroyed but only changed from one form to another.

conduction: The passage of energy, particularly heat or electricity, through something.

GLOSSARY

constellation: A star pattern identified and named as a definite group; usually thought of as forming certain shapes or figures in a specific region of the sky.

consumer: An organism that feeds on other organisms for food.

contrast: A difference, or something that is different, compared with something else.

controlled variable (kept the same): The conditions that are kept the same in a scientific investigation.

convection: Circulatory movement in a liquid or gas, resulting from regions of different temperatures and different densities rising and falling in response to gravity; heat transfer within the atmosphere involving the upward movement of huge volumes of warm air, leading to subsequent condensation and cloud formation.

core: The central part of Earth, or the corresponding part of another celestial body.

crest: The peak or highest point on a wave.

crust: The thin outermost layer of Earth, approximately one percent of Earth's volume, that varies in thickness and has a different composition than the interior.

decomposer: Any organism that feeds or obtains nutrients by breaking down organic matter from dead plants and animals.

density: A measure of a quantity such as mass or electric charge per unit volume.

dependent variable: Factor being measured or observed in an experiment.

depostion: Layering matter in a natural process.

description: A written or verbal account, representation, or explanation of something.

dew: Moisture from the air that has condensed as tiny drops on outdoor objects and surfaces that have cooled, especially during the night.

dew point: The temperature at which the air cannot hold all the moisture in it and dew begins to form.

diffraction: The change in direction of a wave caused by passing by an obstacle or traveling through an opening.

digest: To process food in the body of a living organism into a form that can be absorbed and used or excreted.

digestive system: The system by which ingested food is acted upon by physical and chemical means to provide the body with absorbable nutrients and to excrete waste products; in mammals the system includes the alimentary canal extending from the mouth to the anus, and the hormones and enzymes assisting in digestion.

digestive gland: Any gland having ducts that pour secretions into the digestive tract, such as the salivary glands, liver, and pancreas.

dominance: Tendency of certain (dominant) alleles to mask the expression of their corresponding (recessive) alleles.

earthquake: The shaking of the ground caused by a sudden release of energy in Earth's crust.

GLOSSARY

eclipse: In astronomy, partial or total obscuring of one celestial body by the shadow of another. Best known are the lunar eclipses, which occur when Earth blocks the sun's light from the moon, and solar eclipses, occurring when the moon blocks the sun's light from a small portion of Earth.

ecosystem: An integrated unit of a biological community, its physical environment, and interactions.

efficiency: The relative effectiveness of a system or device determined by comparing input and output.

electromagnetic radiation: The emission and propagation of the entire range of electromagnetic spectrum including: gamma rays, x-rays, ultraviolet radiation, visible light, microwaves, and radio waves.

electron: An elementary particle with a negative electrical charge.

electron shell: The nucleus of an atom is surrounded by negatively charged electrons. The electrons are arranged in layers or shells. An atom can have as many as seven shells, each of which holds only a certain number of electrons.

element: Substance that cannot be broken down into simpler chemical substances.

energy: A quantity that describes the capacity to do work; a source of usable power.

energy pyramid: A pyramidal diagram that compares the amount of energy available at each position, or level, in the feeding order.

energy transfer: A change of energy from one form to another (e.g., mechanical to electrical, solar to electrical).

entropy: A measure of randomness or disorder of a closed system.

environment: The air, water, minerals, organisms, and all other external factors surrounding and affecting a given organism at any time; external factors influencing the life of organisms, such as light or food supply.

equator: An imaginary circle around Earth's surface located between the poles and a plane perpendicular to its axis of rotation that divides it into the Northern and Southern Hemispheres.

erosion: A combination of natural processes in which materials from Earth's surface are loosened, dissolved, or worn away and transported from one place to another.

evaporation: The process by which a liquid is converted to its vapor phase by heating the liquid.

evidence: Something that gives a sign or proof of the existence or truth of something, or that helps somebody to come to a particular conclusion.

evolution: A concept that embodies the belief that existing animals and plants developed by a process of gradual, continuous change from previously existing forms.

experiment: A procedure that is carried out and repeated under controlled conditions in order to discover, demonstrate, or test a hypothesis: includes all components of the scientific method.

GLOSSARY

extinct (in biology): Disappearance of species of living organisms as a result of changed conditions to which the species is not suited. If no member of the affected species survives and reproduces, the entire line dies out, leaving no descendants.

factor: One of the elements contributing to a particular result or situation; any of certain substances necessary to a biochemical or physiological process, such as, blood clotting.

fat: Any of several white or yellowish greasy substances, forming the chief part of adipose tissue of animals and also occurring in plants, that when pure are colorless, odorless, and tasteless and are either solid or liquid esters of glycerol with fatty acids; a greasy water-insoluble solid or semisolid chemical compound that is among the chief nutritional components of food.

filter: A separating medium or device for removing small particles from a gas or liquid by mechanical interception, based mainly on the difference between the size of the particles and the openings in the filter medium, but sometimes also aided by electrostatic forces; any porous layer or material, such as sand, paper, or cloth, used in or as a filter.

food chain: Transfer of energy through various stages as a result of feeding patterns of a series of organisms.

food web (food cycle): The interconnected feeding relationships in a food chain found in a particular place and time.

force: A quality that tends to produce movement or acceleration of a body in the direction of its application; a push or pull.

fossil: A whole or part of a plant or animal that has been preserved in sedimentary rock.

fossil fuels: The remains of animal or plant life from past geologic ages that are now in a form suitable for use as a fuel (e.g., oil, coal, or natural gas).

frequency: The number of times that something such as an oscillation, a waveform, or a cycle is repeated within a particular length of time, usually one second. Symbol: F

friction: A force that opposes the relative motion of two material surfaces in contact with one another.

frictional force: Resistance offered to the movement of one body past another body with which it is in contact.

fulcrum: The pivot point of a lever.

galaxy: A large collection of stars, gases, and dust that are part of the universe (e.g., the Milky Way galaxy) bound together by gravitational forces.

gas: One of the fundamental states of matter in which the molecules do not have a fixed volume or shape.

gender: The sex of a person or organism, or of a whole category of people or organisms.

gene: The basic unit capable of transmitting characteristics from one generation to the next. It consists of a specific sequence of DNA or RNA that occupies a fixed position (locus) on a chromosome.

GLOSSARY

genetic: Involving, resulting from, or relating to genes or genetics.

germination: To start to grow from a seed or spore into a new organism.

gravitation: A force of attraction between two masses.

gravity: The observed effect of the force of gravitation.

groundwater: Water flowing underground in soil or permeable rock, often feeding springs and wells.

habitat: A place in an ecosystem where an organism normally lives.

heat (thermal) energy: A transfer of energy from one part of a substance to another, or from one object to another, because of a difference in temperature. Heat is a form of energy associated with the motion of atoms or molecules and is capable of being transmitted through solid and fluid media by conduction, through fluid media by convection, and through empty space by radiation.

heribivore: An animal that feeds on plants.

herbicide: A chemical preparation designed to kill plants, especially weeds, or to inhibit their growth.

heterozygous: Cell or organism that has two different alleles for a particular trait.

homozygous: Cell or organism that has identical rather than different alleles for a particular trait.

hypothesis: In an experiment, an explanation for a question or a problem that can be formally tested; a prediction with a cause/effect reason.

inclined plane: A type of simple machine; a slanted surface that makes it easier to move a mass from a lower point to a higher point.

igneous: Rock formed under conditions of intense heat or produced by the solidification of volcanic magma on or below the Earth's surface.

image: The likeness of somebody or something that appears in a mirror, through a lens, or on the retina of the eye, or that is produced electronically on a screen.

independent variable: The factor that is changed in an experiment in order to study changes in the dependent variable.

inertia: The property of an object, due to its mass, by which it resists any change in its position unless overcome by force.

insoluble: Incapable of being dissolved in a liquid.

interpret: To establish or explain the meaning or significance of something.

intestine: Part of the digestive system that digests and absorbs food.

GLOSSARY

investigation: A procedure that is carried out in order to observe a response caused by a stimulus; not a complete experiment.

issue: A topic for discussion or of general concern.

kinetic energy: The energy that a body or system has because of its motion.

landform: A natural physical feature of Earth's surface, ranging from large-scale features such as plains, plateaus, and mountains to minor features such as hills and valleys.

landmass: A very large unbroken area of land (for example, a continent or large island).

landslide: The collapse of part of a mountainside or cliff so that it descends in a disintegrating mass of rocks and earth.

lever: A type of simple machine; consists of a rigid bar that pivots about a fulcrum, used to transmit and enhance power or motion.

life cycle: The entire sequence of events in an organism's growth and development.

light: Electromagnetic radiation that lies within the visible range.

liquid: One of the fundamental states of matter with a definite volume but no definite shape.

leverage: The mechanical advantage gained by using a lever.

lunar: Relating to a moon or its movement around a planet, especially the moon in relation to Earth.

luster of minerals: The quality and amount of light reflected from the surface of a mineral.

magnetic: Having the property of attracting iron and certain other materials by virtue of a surrounding field of force.

magnetic field: The region where magnetic force exists around magnets or electric currents.

magnetic pole: Two nearly opposite ends of the planet where Earth's magnetic intensity is the greatest, as the north and south magnetic poles.

magnetism: Force of attraction or repulsion between various substances, especially those made of iron and certain other metals; ultimately it is due to the motion of electric charges.

manipulated (changed) variable: The factor of a system being investigated that is deliberately changed to determine that factor's relationship to the responding variable.

mantle: The part of Earth or another planet that lies between the crust and core.

mass: The amount of matter an object contains.

matter: A solid, liquid, or gas that possesses inertia and is capable of occupying space.

GLOSSARY

meiosis: The process of nuclear division in cells during which the number of chromosomes is reduced by half.

metamorphic: Sedimentary or igneous rocks that have been transformed by heat, pressure, or both; usually formed deep within Earth, during a process such as mountain building.

microorganism: A tiny organism such as a virus, protozoan, or bacterium that can only be seen under a microscope.

microscope: A device that uses a lens or system of lenses to produce a greatly magnified image of a small object.

millimeter (mm): A unit of length equal to one-thousandth of a meter.

mitosis: A process of nuclear division in eukaryotic cells during which the nucleus of a cell divides into two nuclei, each with the same number of chromosomes.

mixture: A substance containing several ingredients combined or blended together.

moon: A natural satellite that revolves around a planet.

moon phase: A phrase that indicates the fraction of the Moon's disc that is illuminated (as seen from Earth); the eight moon phases (in order): new moon, waxing crescent, first quarter, waxing gibbous, full moon, waning gibbous, last quarter, waning crescent.

natural selection: The process, according to Darwin, by which organisms best suited to survival in a particular environment achieve greater reproductive success, thereby passing advantageous genetic characteristics on to future generations.

neap tide: A twice-monthly tide of minimal range that occurs when the Sun, Moon, and Earth are at right angles to each other, thus decreasing the total tidal force exerted on Earth.

nerves: A bundle of fibers forming a network that transmits messages, in the form of impulses, between the brain or spinal cord and the body's organs.

neutral: A particle, object, or system that lacks a net charge.

neutron: Uncharged elementary particle of slightly greater mass than the proton.

nitrogen: A nonmetallic chemical element that occurs as a colorless, odorless, almost inert gas and makes up 4/5 of Earth's atmosphere by volume. Symbol: N

nonrenewable resource: A resource that can only be replenished over millions of years.

nucleus: The positively charged central region of an atom, consisting of protons and neutrons and containing most of the mass; the central body, usually spherical, within a eukaryotic cell, which is a membrane-encased mass of protoplasm containing the chromosomes and other genetic information necessary to control cell growth and reproduction.

GLOSSARY

ocean basin: A depression on the surface of Earth occupied by water.

opinion: A conclusion drawn from observation of the facts.

organ: A complete and independent part of a plant or animal that has a specific function.

organic: Relating to, derived from, or characteristic of living things.

organism: Any living plant, animal, or fungus that maintains various vital processes necessary for life.

particle: A minute body that is considered to have finite mass but negligible size; any one of the basic units of matter (for example, a molecule, atom, or electron).

pattern: A regular or repetitive form, order, or arrangement.

pesticide: A chemical substance used to kill pests, especially insects.

pH: A measure of the acidity or alkalinity of a solution, such as vinegar, or a damp substance, such as soil.

phenomena: Events or objects occurring in the natural world.

photsynthesis: A chemical process by which plants trap light energy to convert carbon dioxide and water into carbohydrates (sugars).

physical change: A reaction; a change in matter from one form to another, without forming new substances.

planet: A large body in space that orbits a star and does not produce light of its own.

plate tectonics: Theory of global dynamics in which Earth's crust is divided into a smaller number of large, rigid plates whose movements cause seismic activity along their borders.

pollution: Any alteration of the natural environment producing a condition harmful to living organisms; may occur naturally or as a result of human activities.

population: A group of organisms of the same species living in a specific geographical area.

potential energy: The energy that a body or system has stored because of its position in an electric, magnetic, or gravitational field, or because of its configuration.

predator: A carnivorous animal that hunts, kills, and eats other animals in order to survive, or any other organism that behaves in a similar manner.

GLOSSARY

pressure: The force acting on a surface divided by the area over which it acts. Symbol: p

prey: An animal or animals that are caught, killed, and eaten by another animal as food.

prism: A piece of glass with polished plane surfaces that disperses a beam of white light into its component colors.

producer: An organism that makes its own food from the environment; usually a green plant.

properties: The basic or essential attributes shared by all members of a group.

protein: A complex natural substance that has a high molecular weight and a globular or fibrous structure composed of amino acids linked by peptide bonds; a food source that is rich in protein molecules.

protist: Unicellular organisms belonging to the kingdom of Protista.

proton: Tiny atomic particle that has mass and a positive electrical charge.

pulley: A type of simple machine; a circular lever, usually a wheel with a groove where a rope can be placed and used to change the direction of a force.

Punnett square: A graphic checkboard used to determine results from a particular genetic cross.

radiation: Any kind of energy that is emitted from a source in the form of rays or waves (for example, heat, light, or sound).

reaction: An equal but opposite force exerted by a body when a force acts upon it.

recessive: An allele for a trait that will be masked unless the organism is homozygous for this trait.

recycle: To save or collect used or waste material for reprocessing into something useful.

reflect: To redirect something that strikes a surface, especially light, sound, or heat, usually back toward its point of origin; to show a reverse image on a mirror or other reflective surface.

refraction: A change in direction of a wave that occurs as it passes from one medium to another of different density.

relationship: The connections between systems, subsystems, or parts of systems described by the concepts and principles of science that may range from correlational to causal (cause-effect).

reliable: An attribute of any investigation that describes the consistency of producing the same observations or data.

GLOSSARY

renewable resource: A resource that is replaced or restored, as it is used, by natural processes in a reasonable amount of time.

repel: To exert a force that tends to push something away.

report: To give detailed information about research or an investigation.

resource: A source of supply, support, or aid, especially one that can be readily drawn upon when needed.

respiratory system: The system of organs in the body of an organism responsible for the intake of oxygen and the expiration of carbon dioxide.

responding (dependent) variable: The factor of a system being investigated that changes in response to the manipulated variable and is measured.

reuse: To use something again, often for a different purpose and usually as an alternative to disposing of it as waste.

river system: A river system is a group of interdependent rivers, including a river and its tributaries. For example the Amazon river system includes the Amazon, Negro, and Tocantins rivers. They can be classified according to their stage of development as young, mature, or old. The young river is marked by a steepsided valley, steep gradients, and irregularities in the bed; the mature river by a valley with a wide floor and flaring sides, by advanced headward erosion by tributaries, and by a more smoothly graded bed; and the old river by a course graded to base level and running through a peneplain, or broad flat area.

rock cycle: The web of environmental processes that forms and changes rocks.

scientific method: A plan of inquiry that uses science process skills as tools to gather, organize, analyze, and communicate information.

screw: A type of simple machine that consists of an inclined plane wrapped around a cylinder.

sedimentary: Used to describe rocks formed from material, including debris of organic origin, deposited as sediment by water, wind, or ice and then consolidated by pressure.

sexual reproduction: Reproduction involving the union of gametes producing an offspring with traits from both parents.

GLOSSARY

solar system: The sun and all the planets, satellites, asteroids, meteors, and comets that are subject to its gravitational pull.

solid: Having a definite shape and a definite volume; one of the fundamental states of matter.

solution: A mixture of two or more substances uniformly dispersed throughout a single phase.

soluble: A measure of one substance's ability to dissolve in a specific amount of another substance at standard temperature and pressure.

specialization: The adaptation of an organism or a part of an organism to a particular function or condition in response to environmental conditions.

spectroscope: An instrument that uses a prism to separate and catalog light wavelengths.

speed: Amount of distance traveled divided by time taken; the time-rate at which any physical process takes place.

spherical: A form in the shape of a ball.

spring tide: The tide of increased range that occurs twice monthly at the new and full phases of the Moon.

star: A large, gaseous, self-luminous body held together by gravity and powered by thermonuclear reactions.

state (phase) of matter: Forms of matter differing in several properties because of differences in the motions and forces of the molecules (or atoms, ions, or elementary particles) of which they are composed; three commonly recognized states of matter: solid, liquid, and gas.

stomach: An organ resembling a sac in which food is mixed and partially digested. It forms part of the digestive tract of vertebrates and is situated between the esophagus and the small intestine.

subsystem: A system that forms part of a larger system.

summarize: To make or give a shortened version of something that has been said or written, stating its main points.

sun: The closest star to Earth and the center of our solar system.

system: A set of objects, organisms, or different parts acting to form a whole.

telescope: A device for making distant objects appear nearer and larger by means of compound lenses or concave mirrors.

tissue: Organic body material in animals and plants made up of large numbers of cells that are similar in form and function and their related intercellular substances.

thermal energy: Internal energy found by adding the kinetic energy of particles making up a substance.

GLOSSARY

tissue: Similar cells acting to perform a specific function; four basic types of tissue are muscle, connective, nerve, and epidermal.

topography: The study and mapping of the features on the surface of land, including natural features such as mountains and rivers and constructed features such as highways and railroads.

transfer: The movement of energy from one location in a system to another system or subsystem.

transmit: To transfer power, force, or movement from one part of a mechanism to another; to make heat, sound, light, or other radiation pass or spread through space or a medium; to send a signal by radio waves, satellite, or wire.

transformation: The conversion of a normal cell into a malignant cell brought about by the action of a carcinogen or virus; the change of one type of atom to another, resulting from a nuclear reaction.

tropism: The motion of an organism or part of an organism toward or away from an external stimulus.

trough: The lowest point on a wave.

universe: The total sum of all matter and energy that exists.

validity: An attribute of an investigation that describes the quality of data produced in the investigation; the investigation question is answered with confidence; ensures that the manipulated variable caused the change in the responding or dependent variable.

vein: Any of the blood vessels that carry blood to the heart.

variable: An event, condition, or factor that can be changed or controlled in order to study or test a hypothesis in a scientific experiment.

velocity: The time-rate at which a body changes its position; defined as displacement divided by the time of travel.

vibration: A repetitive movement around an equilibrium point.

virus: A noncellular, disease-causing particle that uses the genetic material from its host to reproduce.

volcano: A vent or fissure in Earth's surface through which magma and its associated materials are expelled; generally a mountain-like structure.

volume: A measure of the amount of space an object takes up; also the loudness of a sound or signal.

warm-blooded: Maintaining a nearly constant body temperature, usually higher than, and independent of, the temperature of the environment.

GLOSSARY

water cycle: The path water takes as it is being cycled through the environment, including condensation, evaporation, and precipitation.

watershed: The land area that drains into a particular lake, river, or ocean.

water table: The upper surface of groundwater, below which pores in the rocks are filled with water.

wavelength: The distance between two points on adjacent waves that have the same phase (for example, the distance between two consecutive peaks or troughs).

weathering: The natural processes that break down and change rock into soil, sand, and other materials; differs from erosion in that no transportation of those materials takes place.

wedge: A type of simple machine that consists of an inclined plane used to separate two objects.

wheel and axle: A type of simple machine that consists of a rod driven through the center of a cylinder that is allowed to rotate freely, yielding a mechanical advantage equal to the cylinder's diameter.

wind: The movement of air.

wind current: The steady flow of air in a particular direction.

wind direction: The horizontal flow of air over Earth's surface in a northerly, southerly, easterly, or westerly pattern.

wind speed: The rate of the motion of the air over a unit of time. The wind speed unit most often used in the United States is miles per hour.

Science
Practice Tutorial

Science Practice Tutorial

Directions for the Science Practice Tutorial

The Science Practice Tutorial contains a Science Reference Sheet, Periodic Table, and 49 practice questions. You may need formulas or the Periodic Table to help you answer some of the questions. You may refer to the Science Reference Sheet (page 37) or the Periodic Table (page 38) as often as you like. You are permitted use of a calculator, and you will mark your answers on the Answer Sheet on pages 163–166 of this workbook. If you don't understand a question, just ask your teacher to explain it to you.

This section will review the Strands, Standards, and Benchmarks used to assess student achievement in the state of Florida. Following the description of each Benchmark, a student strategy to help you answer the question and a sample mathematics practice item is given. Each item gives you an idea of how the Benchmark may be assessed. Review these items to increase your familiarity with FCAT-style multiple-choice, gridded-response, short-response, and extended-response items. Once you have read through this tutorial section, you will be ready to complete the Science Assessment Tests.

Tips for Using a Calculator on the FCAT Science Test

Here are some hints to help you show what you know when you take the Science Practice Tutorial and the Science Assessments:

- Read the problem carefully. Then decide whether or not you need the calculator to help you solve the problem.

- When starting a new problem, always clear your calculator by pressing the clear key.

- If you see an **E** in the display, clear the error before you begin.

- If you see an **M** in the display, clear the memory and the calculator before you begin.

- If the number in the display is not one of the answer choices, check your work. Remember that when computing with certain types of fractions, you may have to round the number in the display.

- Remember, your calculator will NOT automatically perform the algebraic order of operations.

- Calculators might display an incorrect answer if you press the keys too quickly. When working with calculators, use careful and deliberate keystrokes, and always remember to check your answer to make sure that it is reasonable.

- Always check your answer to make sure that you have completed all of the necessary steps.

Don't Forget...

 This symbol appears next to questions that require short written answers. Use about 5 minutes to answer these questions. A complete and correct answer to each of these questions is worth 2 points. A partially correct answer is worth 1 point.

 This symbol appears next to questions that require longer written answers. Use about 10 to 15 minutes to answer these questions. A complete and correct answer to each of these questions is worth 4 points. A partially correct answer is worth 1, 2, or 3 points.

 Science test questions with this symbol require that you fill in a grid on your answer sheet. There may be more than one correct way to fill in a response grid. The gridded-response section on pages 56-57 will show you the different ways the response grid may be completed. You MUST fill in the bubbles accurately to receive credit for your answer. A correct answer to each of these questions is worth 1 point.

Sample Multiple-Choice Item

To help you understand how to answer the test questions, look at the sample test question and Answer Sheet below. It is included to show you what a multiple-choice question in the test is like and how to mark your answer on your Answer Sheet.

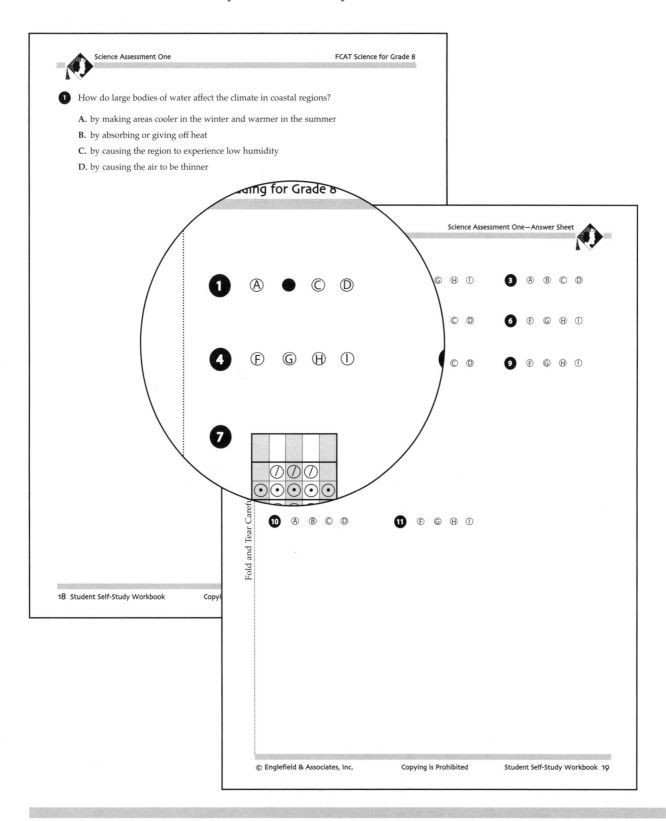

Sample Gridded-Response Item

To help you understand how to answer the test questions, look at the sample test question and Answer Sheet below. It is included to show you what a gridded-response item in the test is like and how to mark your response on your Answer Sheet.

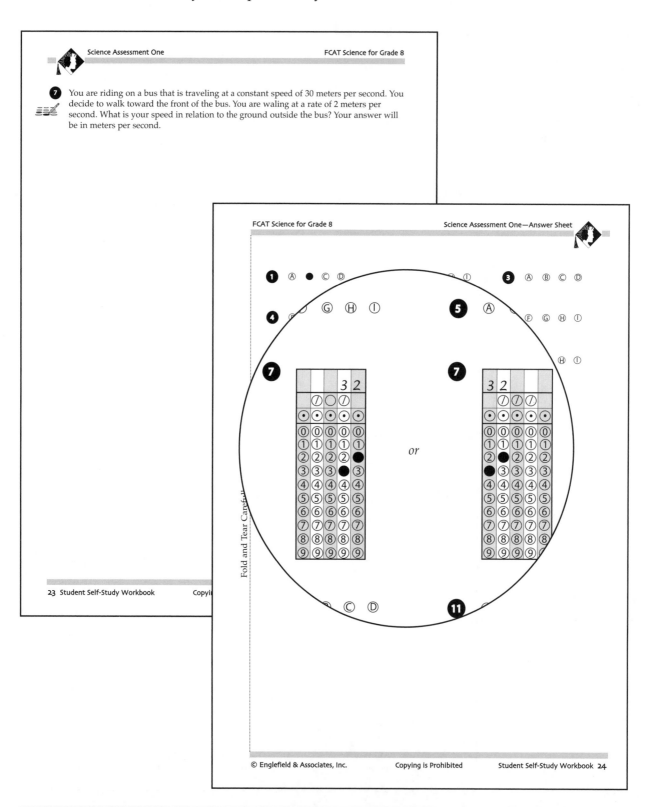

Science Assessment One   FCAT Science for Grade 8

7 You are riding on a bus that is traveling at a constant speed of 30 meters per second. You decide to walk toward the front of the bus. You are waling at a rate of 2 meters per second. What is your speed in relation to the ground outside the bus? Your answer will be in meters per second.

23 Student Self-Study Workbook   Copyi

FCAT Science for Grade 8   Science Assessment One—Answer Sheet

or

Fold and Tear Carefully

© Englefield & Associates, Inc.   Copying is Prohibited   Student Self-Study Workbook 24

Additional Gridded-Response Item Information

Each gridded-response question requires a numerical answer which should be filled into a bubble grid. The bubble grid consists of 5 columns. Each column contains numbers 0–9 and a decimal point; the middle three columns contain a fraction bar as well. You do not need to include any commas for numbers greater than 999. When filling in your answer, only fill in one bubble per column. All gridded-response questions are constructed so the answer will fit into the grid. You can print your answer with the first digit in the left answer box, or with the last digit in the right answer box. Print only one digit or symbol in each answer box. Do not leave a blank box in the middle of an answer. Make sure you fill in a bubble under each box in which you wrote an answer and be sure to write your answer in the grid above the bubbles as well, in case clarification is needed. Answers can be given in whole number, fraction, or decimal form. For questions involving measurements, the unit of measure required for the answer will be provided for you. When a percent is required to answer a question, do NOT convert the percent to its decimal or fractional equivalent. Grid in the percent value without the % symbol. You may NOT write a mixed number such as $13\frac{1}{4}$ in the answer grid. If your answer is a mixed number, you must convert the answer to an improper fraction, such as $\frac{53}{4}$, or to a decimal number, such as 13.25. If you try to fill in $13\frac{1}{4}$, it will be read as $\frac{131}{4}$ and be counted as wrong. You will also be instructed when to round your answer in a particular way. Some example responses are given below.

Answer: 23,901   Answer: 26.5   Answer: 0.071   Answer: $\frac{3}{8}$

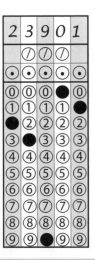 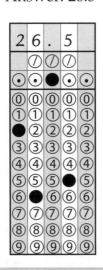 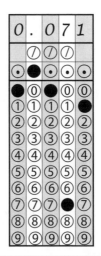

Sample Short-Response Item

To help you understand how to answer the test questions, look at the sample test question below. It is included to show you what a short-response item in the test is like. On the next page is a sample answer to show you how to mark your response on your Answer Sheet.

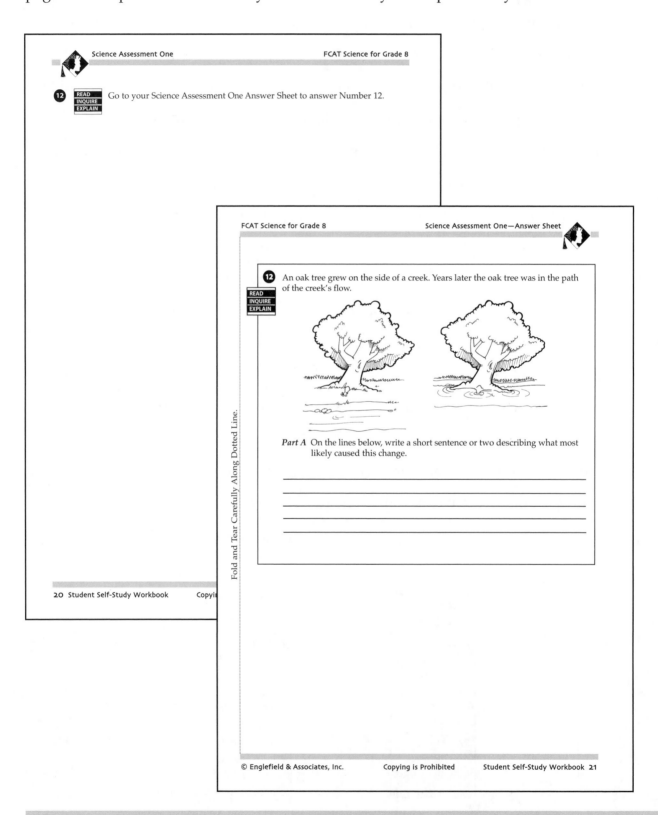

Answer Sheet for Sample Short-Response Item

This is a sample Answer Sheet with the answer included to show you how to mark your response on the test.

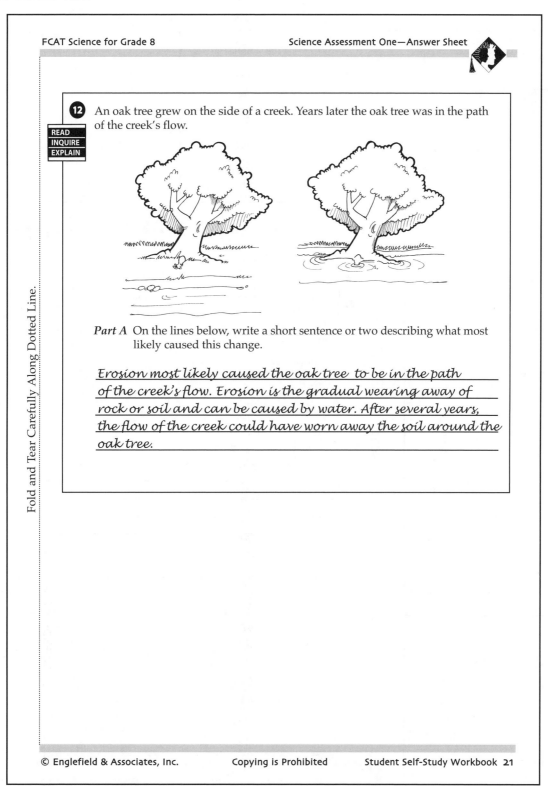

FCAT Science for Grade 8   Science Assessment One—Answer Sheet

12 An oak tree grew on the side of a creek. Years later the oak tree was in the path of the creek's flow.

READ
INQUIRE
EXPLAIN

Part A On the lines below, write a short sentence or two describing what most likely caused this change.

Erosion most likely caused the oak tree to be in the path of the creek's flow. Erosion is the gradual wearing away of rock or soil and can be caused by water. After several years, the flow of the creek could have worn away the soil around the oak tree.

Fold and Tear Carefully Along Dotted Line.

© Englefield & Associates, Inc.   Copying is Prohibited   Student Self-Study Workbook 21

Sample Extended-Response Item

To help you understand how to answer the test questions, look at the sample test question below. It is included to show you what an extended-response item in the test is like. On the next page is a sample answer to show you how to mark your response on your Answer Sheet.

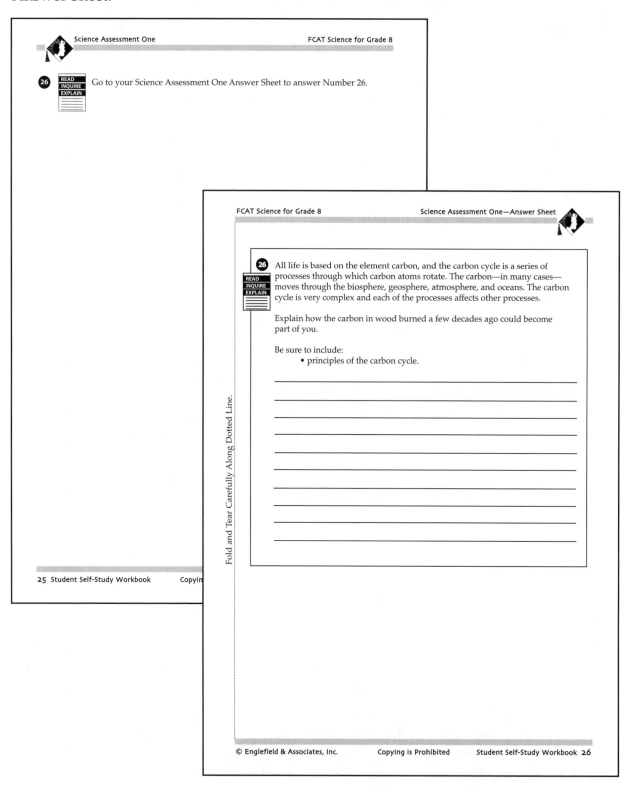

Science Assessment One

FCAT Science for Grade 8

26 **READ INQUIRE EXPLAIN** Go to your Science Assessment One Answer Sheet to answer Number 26.

FCAT Science for Grade 8

Science Assessment One—Answer Sheet

26 **READ INQUIRE EXPLAIN** All life is based on the element carbon, and the carbon cycle is a series of processes through which carbon atoms rotate. The carbon—in many cases—moves through the biosphere, geosphere, atmosphere, and oceans. The carbon cycle is very complex and each of the processes affects other processes.

Explain how the carbon in wood burned a few decades ago could become part of you.

Be sure to include:
  • principles of the carbon cycle.

Fold and Tear Carefully Along Dotted Line.

25 Student Self-Study Workbook   Copyin

© Englefield & Associates, Inc.   Copying is Prohibited   Student Self-Study Workbook 26

Answer Sheet for Sample Extended-Response Item

This is a sample Answer Sheet with the answer included to show you how to mark your response on the test.

FCAT Reading for Grade 8   Science Assessment One—Answer Sheet

26 All life is based on the element carbon, and the carbon cycle is a series of processes through which carbon atoms rotate. The carbon—in many cases—moves through the biosphere, geosphere, atmosphere, and oceans. The carbon cycle is very complex and each of the processes affects other processes.

Explain how the carbon in wood burned a few decades ago could become part of you.

Be sure to include:
  • principles of the carbon cycle.

Wood from a tree that is living contains carbon atoms. When the tree is cut down and the wood is burned, carbon dioxide is given off and exists in the atmosphere. A living plant would then take that carbon dioxide in and, through photosynthesis, the plant would sustain itself. If a human being then ate that plant, the human being would be taking in carbon atoms that once were present in the wood that was burned. The carbon becomes part of the human.

Fold and Tear Carefully Along Dotted Line.

© Englefield & Associates, Inc.   Copying is Prohibited   Student Self-Study Workbook 26

How to Answer the "Read, Inquire, Explain" Questions

Answers to the short- and extended-response problems can receive full or partial credit. You should try to answer these questions even if you are not sure of the correct answer. If a portion of the answer is correct, you will get a portion of the points.

- Allow about 5 minutes to answer the short "Read, Inquire, Explain" questions and about 10 to 15 minutes to answer the long questions.

- Read the question carefully.

- If you do not understand the question, read and answer one part at a time.

- Be sure to answer every part of the question.

- Use the information provided to answer the question.

- Show your work. This shows that you understand how to solve the problem.

- Write explanations in clear, concise language. Use only the space provided on the Answer Sheet. Be sure to keep your writing or drawings inside the box.

- Reread your explanation to make sure it says what you want it to say.

Additional Hints to Remember for Taking the FCAT Science Test

Here are some hints to help you do your best when you take the FCAT Science test. Keep these hints in mind when you answer the sample questions.

- Learn how to answer each kind of question. The FCAT Science test for Grade 8 has four types of questions: multiple-choice, gridded-response, short-response, and extended-response.

- Read each question carefully and think about ways to solve the problem before you try to answer the question.

- Answer the questions you are sure about first. If a question seems too difficult, skip it and go back to it later.

- Be sure to fill in the answer bubbles correctly. Do not make any stray marks around answer spaces.

- Think positively. Some questions may seem hard to you, but you may be able to figure out what to do if you read each question carefully.

- When you have finished each question, reread it to make sure your answer is reasonable.

- Relax. Some people get nervous about tests. It's natural. Just do your best.

Question **1** *assesses:*

Strand A: The Nature of Matter

Standard 1: The student understands that all matter has observable, measurable properties.

SC.A.1.3.1 The student identifies various ways in which substances differ (e.g., mass, volume, shape, density, texture, and reaction to temperature and light). [Also assesses: SC.A.1.3.2 The student understands the difference between weight and mass. SC.A.1.3.6 The student knows that equal volumes of different substances may have different masses.]

Student Strategies:

Substances can differ from each other in a variety of observable ways. You may be able to observe differences in color, size, shape, or texture merely by looking at two objects. Other differences may need to be measured. For example, the mass of an object is the measurement of how much material an object has. You would measure the mass of an object with a balance scale that gives the measurement in grams. The weight of an object can also be measured by a scale, but while the mass of an object remains the same no matter the location of the object, the weight of an object is a measure of the pull of gravity on the object, and can change depending on the location. Weight is usually measured in newtons, since it is a measure of the force of gravity. Objects are also commonly defined by weight in terms of pounds.

The volume of an object is a measure of how much space it takes up. Volume is measured in units of liters for liquids and cubic centimeters for solids. An object's density is a measurement of its mass divided by its volume. Therefore, a dense object will take up less volume than another object that is less dense but has the same mass. For example, iron is denser than wood, so a gram of iron will be smaller, or take up less volume, than a gram of wood.

---

1   Imagine that you have two cubes of different unknown materials. The cubes are exactly the same in size, shape, and volume. You are conducting experiments in order to determine information about the cubes. You place the first cube in water and it floats. What can you expect the second cube to do in water?

A. It will float.
B. It will sink.
C. It will float only if its size does not change.
D. You cannot know what the second cube will do.

Go On ▶

Analysis: Choice D is correct. The density of an object determines whether or not it floats. The cubes are the same shape and size, but nothing is known about their densities. Choices A, B, and C are incorrect because they require knowledge of the cube's density.

Question **2** *assesses:*

Strand A: The Nature of Matter

> **Standard 1: The student understands that all matter has observable, measurable properties.**
>
> > **SC.A.1.3.3** The student knows that temperature measures the average energy of motion of the particles that make up the substance.

Student Strategies:

Kinetic energy is the energy of motion. You should understand that although objects may appear solid, all matter is made of particles that are too small to be seen. Because these particles are bumping into each other very rapidly, they give the object they make up kinetic energy. The kinetic energy of an object increases if energy, such as heat, is transferred to the object. If the object loses energy, the motion of the particles that make it up slows down and it loses kinetic energy.

2 You are given two unknown liquids and are asked to determine which one's molecules have the higher average kinetic energy. Since directly measuring the kinetic energy of molecules is very difficult, what should you measure in order to determine which of the two liquids has the **higher** average kinetic energy?

    F. density
    G. temperature
    H. weight
    I. mass

Go On ▶

Analysis: Choice G is correct. Temperature is a measure of average kinetic energy of molecules. Choices F, H, and I are all incorrect because they are all measurements of physical characteristics that do not depend on or reflect kinetic energy.

Question **3** *assesses:*

Strand A: The Nature of Matter

> **Standard 1:The student understands that all matter has observable, measurable properties.**
>
> > **SC.A.1.3.4** The student knows that atoms in solids are close together and do not move around easily; in liquids, atoms tend to move farther apart; in gas, atoms are quite far apart and move around freely.

Student Strategies:

Recall that an object is made up of molecules that are in motion and constantly bumping into each other. Remember that the speed and motion of an object's molecules also determine its physical state. As the kinetic energy of its molecules increase, an object may change from a solid to a liquid, or from a liquid to a gas. In reverse, if the molecules' speed slows down, a gas may change to a liquid, or a liquid may change to a solid. As the energy and speed of the molecules increase, they move more rapidly, bump into each other harder and faster, and bounce further away from each other.

Visualize water molecules in your mind. You have seen water boil and become steam. The added heat energy increases the speed and distance between the water molecules until the water expands to become a gas. You have also probably seen water vapor condense into a liquid. The water vapor molecules lose energy and move closer together until liquid water forms.

3 When a solid melts, it changes from a solid to a liquid. As this change occurs, which of the following does **not** happen to the molecules?

A. Their average kinetic energy increases.
B. Their average motion increases.
C. They form new bonds between molecules.
D. They become less closely packed.

Go On ▶

Analysis: Choice C is correct. New molecular bonds do not form as a solid becomes a liquid. It changes form and increases in temperature. As temperature increases, both average kinetic energy and average molecular motion increase, so Choices A and B are incorrect. As a change from solid to liquid occurs, molecules become more widely spaced, so Choice D is incorrect.

Question **4** *assesses:*

Strand A: The Nature of Matter

Standard 1:The student understands that all matter has observable, measurable properties.

SC.A.1.3.5 The student knows the difference between a physical change in a substance (i.e., altering the shape, form, volume, or density) and a chemical change (i.e., producing new substances with different characteristics).

Student Strategies:

Substances can experience many different types of changes. A chemical change is a change in the chemical composition of a substance. Chemical changes affect a substance at the molecular level and usually create a different substance with different characteristics. A physical change is a change that does not affect a substance chemically, but instead alters a physical characteristic of the substance.

If you are unsure whether a substance has experienced a physical change or a chemical change, it is best to examine the substance before and after the change. Ask yourself if the change has created a substance that acts differently from the original substance. Usually a physical change creates a substance that looks a little different, but you can still recognize the original substance. A chemical change typically creates a new substance that acts very different from the original substance.

4 Which of the following shows a chemical change occurring?

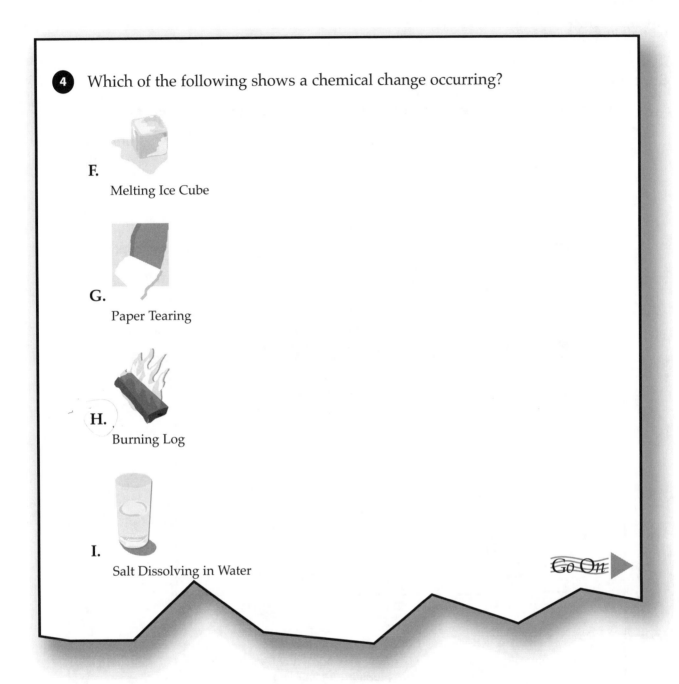

F.
Melting Ice Cube

G.
Paper Tearing

H.
Burning Log

I.
Salt Dissolving in Water

Go On ▶

Analysis: *Choice H is correct. A burning log is chemically changed into ashes. A chemical change is a change in which a new substance is produced. Choice F is incorrect because water is the same substance as ice, simply in a new form. Choice G is incorrect because torn paper is still paper, just in a different shape. Choice I is incorrect because the water and salt remain the same molecules, they are now just mixed together.*

Question **5** *assesses:*

Strand A: The Nature of Matter

Standard 2: The student understands the basic principles of atomic theory.

SC.A.2.3.1 The student describes and compares the properties of particles and waves.

Student Strategies:

You should understand that matter and energy move in waves. The waves that transfer energy and motion are very similar to the waves on the ocean. They have a high point, or crest, and a low point, or trough. A typical wave is shown below.

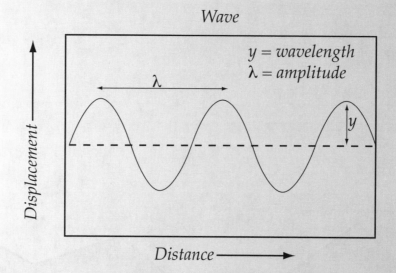

Wave

$y = wavelength$
$\lambda = amplitude$

Waves can move substances or energy. Waves that move energy can exist in a vacuum, with no material at all. Waves can be measured according to their size or their movement. The properties of waves change as they go through different mediums or substances. You encounter waves in various forms every day. For example, sound waves are interpreted by your ears as sound, and energy waves heat the Earth and cook your food.

Particles refer to an individual component of an object or energy. For example, an atom is made up of particles such as protons, electrons, and neutrons that are bound together by electrical charges.

5 Particles and waves have many similarities and many differences. Which of the following is a characteristic of both waves and particles?

A. mass
B. charge
C. refraction
D. speed

Go On ▶

Analysis: Choice D is correct. Both waves and particles have given speeds. Choice A is incorrect because waves do not have mass. Choice B is incorrect because waves do not have a charge. Choice C in incorrect because particles do not demonstrate refraction.

Question **6** *assesses:*

Strand A: The Nature of Matter

Standard 2: The student understands the basic principles of atomic theory.

SC.A.2.3.2 The student knows the general properties of the atom (a massive nucleus of neutral neutrons and positive protons surrounded by a cloud of negative electrons) and accepts that single atoms are not visible.

Student Strategies:

All matter is made up of atoms. An atom is the smallest amount of any specific type of matter that can exist. Different chemical elements are made up of atoms that have different amounts of smaller subatomic particles that give them their different characteristics. There are three types of subatomic particles that make up an atom.

Electrons are negatively charged and have the least amount of mass. They move in an orbit cloud at very high speeds around the center of the atom.

Protons are positively charged and much more massive than electrons. They can be found in the center, or nucleus, of the atom.

Neutrons have no charge and are slightly more massive than protons. They are also found in the nucleus of the atom.

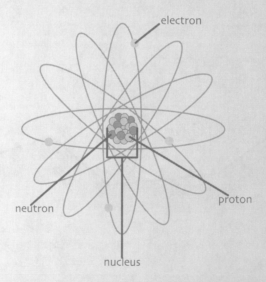

You should be familiar with how the subatomic particles affect the characteristics of an atom. The number of protons and neutrons determines an atom's charge. The number of outer shell electrons determine how an atom reacts with other atoms.

6 Elements have many characteristics that make them unique. One of these characteristics is that the atom has no net charge. This is determined by the relative amounts of certain parts of the atom. Which atomic components keep the atom electrically neutral?

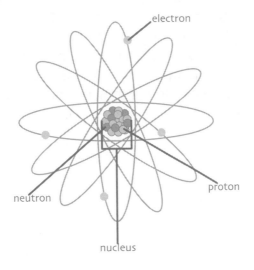

F. protons and neutrons
G. protons and electrons
H. electrons and neutrons
I. neutrons and nucleus

Go On ▶

Analysis: Choice G is correct. A neutral atom has equal numbers of positively charged components (protons) and negatively charged components (electrons). Choice F is incorrect because it does not consider the negative charges. Choice H is incorrect because it does not include the positive charges. Choice I is incorrect because it does not consider the negative charges (the protons are a part of the nucleus).

Question **7** *assesses:*

Strand B: Energy

Standard 1: The student recognizes that energy may be changed in form with varying efficiency.

SC.B.1.3.1 The student identifies forms of energy and explains that they can be measured and compared. [Also assesses: A.2.3.3 The student knows that radiation, light, and heat are forms of energy used to cook food, treat diseases, and provide energy. B.1.3.2 The student knows that energy cannot be created or destroyed, but only changed from one form to another. SC.B.1.3.3 The students knows that various forms in which energy comes to Earth from the sun (e.g., visible light, infrared, and microwave).]

Student Strategies:

Energy can exist as potential energy or kinetic energy. Kinetic energy is the energy of motion, while potential energy is energy due to an object's position that can be released at some future point. You can imagine kinetic energy as a ball rolling down a hill. In that example, the ball's energy is released through its motion. However, if the ball sits at the top of the hill, it has potential energy. The potential energy is due to the position of the ball and the force that gravity exerts on it.

Kinetic energy can be expressed by a formula:

$$\text{Kinetic energy} = 1/2 \text{ mass} \times \text{speed}^2$$

Potential energy can be calculated based on the amount of work that can be done by the object. To calculate this, you need to know the mass of the object and the distance it moves. Other sources of potential energy include potential chemical energy and potential electrical energy. An object exposed to pressure, such as a stretched rubber band or a diving board, also has potential energy.

7 An object can have many different types of energy, which are determined by various factors. Which of the following is important to **both** an object's kinetic energy and its potential energy?

A. speed
B. mass
C. size
D. height

Go On ▶

Analysis: Choice B is correct. An object's potential energy is determined by height (or position) and mass, while the object's kinetic energy is determined by speed and mass. Choice A is incorrect because speed is only important to kinetic energy. Choice C is incorrect because size is not important to either form of energy. Choice D is incorrect because height is only important to potential energy.

Question **8** *assesses:*

Strand B: Energy

> **Standard 1: The student recognizes that energy may be changed in form with varying efficiency.**
>
> > **SC.B.1.3.4** The student knows that energy conversions are never 100% efficient (i.e., some energy is transformed to heat and is unavailable for further useful work).

Student Strategies:

Energy conversions are never completely efficient. When you feel the running engine of an automobile, you feel the heat energy being released as waste instead of being transformed into the motion of the car.

Try to visualize energy transformations that are occurring in any given scenario. For example, coal is burned at an electric power plant and transformed into electricity that travels to a house and is converted into sound and light energy by a television that is plugged into the electrical outlet. Energy is lost at each of these transformations. Energy can take many forms, and energy can also be transformed from or into matter as well. If you can map out the path that energy takes, you can often see the places where energy is being transformed into waste products. Keep in mind that since some energy is always wasted when it is transformed, as more transformations occur, more energy will be lost.

8 One of the reasons that there are so many plants on Earth is that they use energy directly from the Sun to produce food. Primary consumers, such as cows that graze on grass, get their energy from plants. There are fewer primary consumers than there are plants because less energy is available to primary consumers than is available to producers.

If there is so much energy available to plants, why isn't all of that energy then available to the primary consumers?

F. The plants store their energy in a form that not all primary consumers can use.
G. When plants use the Sun's energy, some energy is lost because the plants are not completely efficient.
H. The energy from plants is chemical energy, which is destroyed by enzymes in the mouths of consumers.
I. Plants store some of their energy in the soil, and that energy is not available to the consumers.

Go On ▶

Analysis: *Choice G is correct. The energy at one level is not entirely available at the next level because no energy conversion is completely efficient. Choice F is incorrect because the energy stored by plants is the same basic form that primary consumers use. Choice H is incorrect because enzymes help release energy, not destroy it. Choice I is incorrect because plants do not store energy outside of themselves.*

Question **9** *assesses:*

Strand B: Energy

Standard 1: The student recognizes that energy may be changed in form with varying efficiency.

SC.B.1.3.5 The student knows the processes by which thermal energy tends to flow from a system of higher temperature to a system of lower temperature.

Student Strategies:

Recall that all objects are made of molecules that are in motion. The motion, or kinetic energy, of molecules in a substance is also known as its thermal energy. Thermal energy can be measured by finding the temperature of the object.

Thermal energy tends to spread out to create equilibrium. That is why when you place a space heater in a room, the heat from the space heater does not stay in front of the heater, but eventually spreads out throughout the room. Thermal energy moves from areas of high thermal energy to areas of low thermal energy. Thinking about it more simply: thermal energy moves from hot areas to colder areas to create equilibrium. Remember that when you are considering these concepts that the terms "hot" and "cold" are relative. Even very cold environments or objects have thermal energy. For example, thermal energy would flow from your refrigerator into your freezer if you made a hole between the two spaces.

9 If you leave an ice cube out on a kitchen table, it will slowly melt into water. If you hold the same ice cube in your hand, it will melt **faster**. Why?

    A. The energy from your hand flows to the ice cube.
    B. Your skin cells contain enzymes that speed up the melting process.
    C. Ice melts slower when the air keeps the surface molecules moving.
    D. Your hand is physically scraping off the ice's surface molecules.

Go On ▶

Analysis: Choice A is correct. The ice melts faster in your hand because of the transfer of heat from your hand to the ice. Choice B is incorrect because there are no enzymes transferred from the hand to the ice in this situation. Choice C is incorrect because the air does not move the ice's surface molecules. Choice D is incorrect because the hand causes the ice to melt as thermal energy flows from the hand to the ice.

Question **10** *assesses:*

Strand B: Energy

Standard 1: The student recognizes that energy may be changed in form with varying efficiency.

SC.B.1.3.6 The student knows the properties of waves (e.g., frequency, wavelength, and amplitude); that each wave consists of a number of crests and troughs; and the effects of different media on waves. [Also assesses: SC.C.1.3.2 The student knows that vibrations in materials set up wave disturbances that spread away from the source (e.g., sound and earthquake waves).]

Student Strategies:

Make sure you are familiar with the structure and properties of waves.

This wave is moving in this direction. ⟶

Wavelength   *Peaks*

Amplitude   *Troughs*

One complete cycle

Visualize the wave as shown above moving through a medium represented by the black horizontal line. The period from one peak to the next makes up one complete wavelength, or cycle. The number of cycles a wave moves through in a given unit of time is its frequency. The amplitude of a wave is the distance from the undisturbed medium (shown by the black line) to the top, or bottom of the wave.

Remember that waves represent the movement of many types of energy. This energy may move through a medium, for example, sound waves move through the air or water or earthquake waves move through the earth. Waves may also move energy without a medium, for example light moves through empty space. The amplitudes, frequency, and wavelengths all affect the properties of the wave. For example, light energy appears as different colors depending on the wavelength of the light waves. These properties can also change when a wave moves between different mediums.

10 Imagine that you are standing against the wall of a building. You are standing a few meters from the corner of the building. You cannot see what is around the corner, but you can hear it. What property of sound waves lets you hear around the corner?

F. diffraction
G. reflection
H. refraction
I. amplitude

Go On ▶

Analysis: *Choice F is correct. Diffraction is the bending of a wave around a barrier. Choice G is incorrect because reflection is the bouncing of a wave off a surface. Choice H is incorrect because refraction is the bending of a wave as it passes from one medium to another. Choice I is incorrect because amplitude is the measure of the size of a wave.*

Question **11** *assesses:*

Strand B: Energy

Standard 2: The student understands the interaction of matter and energy.

SC.B.2.3.1 The student knows that most events in the universe (e.g., weather changes, moving cars, and the transfer of a nervous impulse in the human body) involve some form of energy transfer and that these changes almost always increase the total disorder of the system and its surroundings, reducing the amount of useful energy.

Student Strategies:

You should be familiar with the concept of entropy. Entropy is the amount of energy present in the universe that is not useful for doing work. Most events require energy and when energy is used, the transformation of energy is not completely efficient, so some energy is always transformed in a wasteful way. The increase of wasted, useless energy contributes to entropy. Put more simply, entropy which represents disorder in the universe is constantly increasing, so the universe is constantly becoming more disorganized.

11 Entropy is a measure of the disorder, or randomness, of the universe. What is **true** about the universe's entropy?

    A. It is always increasing.
    B. It is always decreasing.
    C. It is always constant.
    D. It is always both increasing and decreasing.

Go On ▶

Analysis: *Choice A is correct. Every reaction in the universe serves to increase the universe's entropy. Choices B, C, and D are all incorrect because they would violate the second law of thermodynamics, which is that every reaction in the universe serves to increase the universe's entropy.*

Question **12** *assesses:*

Strand C: Force and Motion

Standard 1: The student understands that types of motion may be described, measured, and predicted.

SC.C.1.3.1 The student knows that the motion of an object can be described by its position, direction of motion, and speed.

Student Strategies:

You can describe the motion of an object in many ways. Motion is the change in position of an object over time. You can describe an object's motion by describing the direction and distance of the change in its position. You can also calculate the speed of the motion by dividing the distance over time:

$$\text{Average Speed} = \frac{\text{distance}}{\text{time}}$$

It may be easier to remember that speed, also know as velocity, or rate, is represented by the formula:

d = rt where d = distance, r = rate (or speed or velocity), and t = time.

Notice that with a simple division of both sides of this equation, we get:

$$r = \frac{d}{t}$$ to find speed or rate (the same as the equation above)

or

$$t = \frac{d}{r}$$ to find the time

If an object is slowing down or speeding up, it is accelerating. You can calculate acceleration by dividing the change in speed over time:

$$\text{Acceleration} = \frac{\text{change in speed}}{\text{time}}$$

12 A large bus travels city streets. It takes the bus 10 seconds to cross each city block. If all of the city blocks are the same length, what can be said about the bus?

F. It is accelerating.
G. It is decelerating.
H. It is moving at a constant velocity.
I. It is moving with varying acceleration.

Go On ▶

Analysis: Choice H is correct. The bus is crossing each block in the same amount of time, so the bus is moving at a constant velocity. Choices F, G, and I are all incorrect because the acceleration is constantly zero, so the bus is neither accelerating nor decelerating.

Question **13** *assesses:*

Strand C: Force and Motion

Standard 2: The student understands that the types of force that act on an object and the effect of that force can be described, measured, and predicted.

SC.C.2.3.1 The student knows that many forces (e.g., gravitational, electrical, and magnetic) act at a distance (i.e., without contact).

Student Strategies:

A force is something that causes a change in motion of an object. Forces can either be contact forces, which require contact between two objects, or field forces, which do not require contact.

Examples of contact forces include a hammer hitting a nail or an explosion. Examples of field forces include gravity or magnetic forces.

If you are faced with a question that asks you about force acting on an object, try to visualize what is occurring. You may wish to draw a diagram of the objects and forces involved. Include descriptions of the forces and results involved in your diagram.

Go On ▶

13 Which of the following examples of forces acting on objects requires the objects in question to come into physical contact with one another?

    A. the transfer of motion between balls on a pool table
    B. the falling of a bird's feather toward Earth
    C. the movement of a compass needle to point to the north
    D. the orbiting of the Moon around Earth

Go On ▶

Analysis: Choice A is correct. The mechanical transfer of motion requires physical contact. Choices B and D are incorrect because the effects of gravity do not require physical contact. Choice C is incorrect because magnetism does not require physical contact.

Question **14** *assesses:*

Strand C: Force and Motion

Standard 2: The student understands that the types of force that act on an object and the effect of that force can be described, measured, and predicted.

SC.C.2.3.4 The student knows that simple machines can be used to change the direction or size of a force.

Student Strategies:

You should be familiar with several different types of simple machines.

An inclined plane, such as a ramp, helps you to overcome resistance by moving the object over a larger total distance.

A wedge, such as a door stop, is a type of inclined plane. Instead of moving an object over an inclined plane, however, the wedge moves and the object stays stationary.

A screw is a type of inclined plane that is circular. A screw helps you do work by wedging itself between layers of wood or other material.

A lever allows you to pull or lift objects by pushing on the end of a horizontal arm. The force acts against a pivot, or lever, to lift up at the other end.

A wheel is a type of lever that rotates against an axle and allows you to move things across a distance.

A pulley or a system of pulleys is a wheel that rotates a rope or cord instead of an axle. You pull down on the rope and the pulley transfers the force to an upward motion.

Go On ▶

14 One common simple machine used to lift heavy objects is shown below.

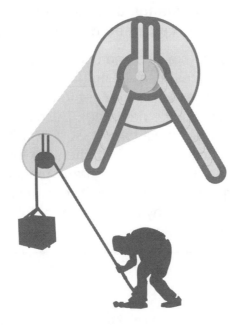

What does this simple machine do to help humans work?

F. It changes the direction of the force.
G. It increases the size of the force.
H. It decreases the size of the force.
I. It changes the timing of the force.

Analysis: *Choice F is correct. A single fixed pulley only changes the direction of the force. A single fixed pulley does not change the size of the force, so Choices G and H are incorrect. A pulley does not change the timing of a force, so Choice I is incorrect.*

Question **15** *assesses:*

Strand C: Force and Motion

Standard 2: The student understands that the types of force that act on an object and the effect of that force can be described, measured, and predicted.

SC.C.2.3.6 The student explains and shows the ways in which a net force (i.e., the sum of all acting forces) can act on an object (e.g., speeding up an object traveling in the same direction as the net force, slowing down an object traveling in the direction opposite of the net force). [Also assesses: SC.C.2.3.2 The student knows common contact forces. SC.C.2.3.3 The student knows that if more than one force acts on an object, then the forces can reinforce or cancel each other, depending on their direction and magnitude. SC.C.2.3.5 The student understands that an object in motion will continue at a constant speed and in a straight line until acted upon by a force and that an object at rest will remain at rest until acted upon by a force.]

Student Strategies:

When determining the affect of one or more forces on an object, you should diagram the direction and relative size of the force to help you determine the result of the force or forces. For example:

A. Your brother is applying force to a bicycle (pedals).

bicycle→

B. You apply additional force to the bicycle (push it back) as your brother is applying force to his bicycle.

you→bicycle→

The bicycle moves forward with the net force (add the forces) that you and your brother are applying to the bicycle. The bicycle moves faster than when he was applying force alone.

C. You apply an equal but opposite force as your brother applies force (pedals).

bicycle→←you

When you add the forces together (equal positive and negative forces) they equal zero. The bicycle does not move.

D. You apply a greater opposite force as your brother applies force (pedals).

you——→←bicycle

When you add the forces together (his small positive force and your greater negative force) they equal a negative number. The bicycle moves backward.

15 You are riding on a bus that is traveling at a constant speed of 30 m/s. You decide to walk toward the front of the bus. You are walking at a rate of 2 m/s.

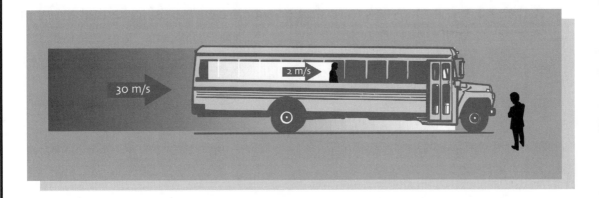

What is your speed in relation to a person standing on the ground outside the bus? 32 M/s

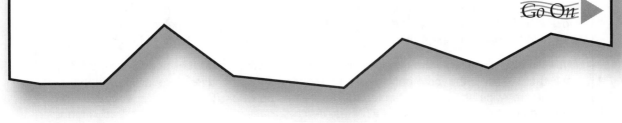

Go On ▶

Analysis: Speed is the time rate at which something is moving along a path. The speed of a person on a bus in relation to the outside ground would be an addition of the two speeds, so the correct answer is 32 m/s.

Question **16** *assesses:*

Strand C: Force and Motion

Standard 2: The student understands that the types of force that act on an object and the effect of that force can be described, measured, and predicted.

SC.C.2.3.7 The student knows that gravity is a universal force that every mass exerts on every other mass.

Student Strategies:

Understanding Gravity

Gravity is such an accepted part of our lives that we rarely think about it even though it affects everything we do. Anytime we drop or throw something and watch it fall to the ground, we see gravity in action. Gravity is the pull that every object exerts on every other object.

Sir Isaac Newton explained in his laws of motion that a moving body continues moving with the same velocity. In other words, its speed and its direction of motion stay the same. The speed or the direction only changes if a force is acting on the body. When you toss a ball into the air, its speed changes; it slows down. Its direction also changes as it starts to fall back to the ground. Newton realized this is due to the force of gravity.

Newton also discovered a number of properties of gravity. The further apart two bodies are, the weaker is the force between them. Gravity obeys the inverse square law: if the bodies are twice as far apart, the force is four times as weak. The force of gravity also depends on the masses of the two bodies. If either mass is doubled, then the force is four times as strong.

Newton's Third Law tells us that the force of gravity is proportional to the size of the masses involved and the distance between them. Because Newton's law affects all objects in the universe, it is therefore known as the Universal Law of Gravitation.

For the FCAT, review the formulas on the Grade 8 FCAT Science Reference Sheet for acceleration, average speed, density, force of motion, momentum, and work found on page 37 of this book.

16 Which of the following **best** describes gravity?

    A. the attraction between all masses
    B. the attraction of a small mass to a large mass
    C. the attraction of a large mass to a small mass
    D. the attraction of living masses to non-living masses

Go On ▶

Analysis: *Choice A is correct. Gravity is the attraction between all masses. Choices B and C are incorrect because gravity's attraction isn't limited to objects with different masses. Choice D is incorrect because gravity affects living and non-living masses equally.*

Question **17** *assesses:*

Strand D: Processes that Shape the Earth

Standard 1: The student recognizes that processes in the lithosphere, atmosphere, hydrosphere, and biosphere interact to shape the Earth.

SC.D.1.3.1 The student knows that mechanical and chemical activities shape and reshape the Earth's land surface by eroding rock and soil in some areas and depositing them in other areas, sometimes in seasonal layers.

Student Strategies:

When you look at Earth's surface, you should recognize the role that erosion and deposition play in changing its shape. Erosion is the wearing down of soil and rock. Deposition occurs when material accumulates in another location. Most erosion and deposition is done by water or wind. Wind is responsible for shaping some of Earth's surface, but wind tends to act more slowly and less dramatically. Water can move materials quickly because it typically has a stronger force and can dissolve minerals and soil. Water can also change state to take on the form of rain, snow, and ice that changes the landscape. For example, large ice glaciers have moved across the continents, like enormous bulldozers, creating flat lands and large lakes.

17 Water affects Earth by shaping Earth's features in a number of ways. Which of the following properties of water is **most** directly involved in at least one type of weathering?

F. Water has high surface tension.
G. Water expands as it freezes.
H. Water has high specific heat.
I. Water boils at a certain point.

Go On ▶

Analysis: Choice G is correct. Of the properties listed, the only one that affects weathering is Choice G. The fact that water expands when it freezes allows it to break apart a rock when water inside a crack freezes. Choices F, H, and I are incorrect because they have little to no effect on weathering.

Question **18** *assesses:*

Strand D: Processes that Shape the Earth

Standard 1: The student recognizes that processes in the lithosphere, atmosphere, hydrosphere, and biosphere interact to shape the Earth.

SC.D.1.3.3 The student knows how conditions that exist in one system influence the conditions that exist in other systems.

Student Strategies:

You should be familiar with all of Earth's systems.

The lithosphere is made up of the crust and upper mantle of Earth. The outer shell of the lithosphere is made up of tectonic plates that move toward, away from, and beside each other.

The atmosphere is made up of the air that surrounds Earth and is held by Earth's gravity.

The hydrosphere is made up of Earth's oceans and all the water that exists on, above, or below Earth's surface.

The biosphere is made up of all the living organisms that inhabit Earth.

When considering a question about Earth's systems, understand that all the systems interact with each other. Processes that occur in one system affect or even cause events to occur in other systems. For example, the heating of air in Earth's atmosphere by the sun causes weather patterns that create storms and other events in the hydrosphere.

 Go On

     © Englefield & Associates, Inc.

18 Climate, weather, and atmosphere are influenced greatly by Earth's physical features, such as mountain ranges. One of the ways that a mountain range is formed is by the movement of tectonic plates.

What causes these mountains to form?

A. Tectonic plates push together.
B. Tectonic plates move apart.
C. New tectonic plates are formed.
D. Old tectonic plates are destroyed.

Analysis: *Choice A is correct. Mountain ranges can be formed when two tectonic plates come together and push upward. Choice B is incorrect because the mountains are forced upward when the plates push together, not when the plates move apart. Choices C and D are incorrect because tectonic plates are not created or destroyed.*

Question **19** *assesses:*

Strand D: Processes that Shape the Earth

Standard 1: The student recognizes that processes in the lithosphere, atmosphere, hydrosphere, and biosphere interact to shape the Earth.

SC.D.1.3.4 The student knows the ways in which plants and animals reshape the landscape (e.g., bacteria, fungi, worms, rodents, and other organisms add organic matter to the soil, increasing soil fertility, encouraging plant growth, and strengthening resistance to erosion). [Also assesses: SC.D.1.3.2 The student knows that over the whole earth, organisms are growing, dying, and decaying as new organisms are produced by the old ones.]

Student Strategies:

Earth's biosphere affects the lithosphere in many ways. The main way that organisms affect the lithosphere is through the relationship that plants have with the soil. Plants hold soil together with their roots. They also cycle nutrients through the soil. Plants create organic carbon by fixing carbon dioxide in the air and converting it to food and organic material. This material is used by many organisms, such as insects and worms, that live in the soil. Almost all organisms contribute organic material to the soil when they die and decompose.

19 Wind is one of the many factors that leads to soil erosion. Wind does not, however, have the same effect in all environments. Soil erosion caused by wind is much more common and significant in a prairie than in a forest. What would explain this?

   F. The grasses that grow in prairies break up the soil, allowing for easier erosion.

   G. The trees in the forest act as a windbreak, reducing the wind's effect.

   H. The trees in the forest keep the Sun from drying the soil.

   I. The prairie soil lacks the nutrients needed to hold it together.

Go On ▶

Analysis: Choice G is correct. Forest trees are able to block the wind and reduce soil erosion. Choice F is incorrect because, although they may be involved in other forms of soil erosion, grass roots would hold the soil together to prevent erosion due to wind. Choice H is incorrect because the dryness of the soil in a forest has only minimal effects on wind erosion. Choice I is incorrect because prairie soil should have a great deal of nutrients and, even if it does not, nutrients are not effective at preventing soil erosion due to wind.

Question **20** *assesses:*

Strand D: Processes that Shape the Earth

Standard 1: The student recognizes that processes in the lithosphere, atmosphere, hydrosphere, and biosphere interact to shape the Earth.

SC.D.1.3.5 The student understands concepts of time and size relating to the interaction of Earth's processes (e.g., lightning striking in a split second as opposed to the shifting of the Earth's plates altering the landscape, distance between atoms measured in Angstrom units as opposed to distance between stars measured in light-years).

Student Strategies:

Earth process are constantly occurring, but they may take very different lengths of time to complete. For example, although Earth's tectonic plates are always in motion, they move very slowly. The processes that occur because of tectonic movement, such as mountain building, generally take hundreds of thousands of years. Erosion activities can happen quickly, as when a flood carries away large amounts of soil, or slowly over thousands or hundreds of thousands of years as when a river erodes soil to create a canyon or ravine.

You should be familiar with different geological or natural events and have an idea of what time span is needed for them to occur. If you aren't sure how long an event needs to happen, you should think about what causes the event. Try to compare how long you think the process would take compared to another process. For example, you know that fossils take a long time to form in rock, but you have probably seen an organism, such as a dead plant, decompose in a matter of days.

20 In which of the following are the events correctly listed from fastest to slowest?

    A. formation of a canyon by erosion, decomposition of a dead tree, light traveling from the Sun to Earth, a signal from the brain causing a muscle contraction

    B. a signal from the brain causing a muscle contraction, light traveling from the Sun to Earth, decomposition of a dead tree, formation of a canyon by erosion

    C. a signal from the brain causing a muscle contraction, formation of a canyon by erosion, light traveling from the Sun to Earth, decomposition of a dead tree

    D. light traveling from the Sun to Earth, decomposition of a dead tree, a signal from the brain causing a muscle contraction, formation of a canyon by erosion

Go On ▶

Analysis: *Choice B is correct. A signal from the brain occurs in less than a second. The light from the Sun reaches Earth in about 8 minutes. The decomposition of a dead tree can take weeks or decades, depending on the environment. The formation of a canyon by erosion would take hundreds, thousands, or millions of years.*

Question **21** *assesses:*

Strand E: Earth and Space

Standard 1: The student understands the interaction and organization in the Solar System and the universe and how this affects life on Earth.

SC.E.1.3.1 The student understands the vast size of our Solar System and the relationship of the planets and their satellites. [Also assesses: SC.E.1.3.2 The student knows that available data from various satellite probes show the similarities and differences among planets and their moons in the Solar System.]

Student Strategies:

The solar system is made up of all the objects that orbit our Sun. The Sun is easily the largest object in the solar system. Below is an image that shows the relative sizes of the planets and the Sun.

The relative sizes of all nine planets in our solar system (distances are not to scale)

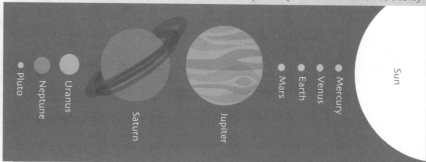

The moons of each planet are much smaller than the planets themselves. Almost all moons are thought to come from the same material as the planets they orbit. Remember that most of the inner planets in our solar system are small and rocky, while most of the outer planets are very large and are made of gases.

21 Which of the following objects in the solar system is the **smallest**?

F. Earth's Moon
G. Pluto
H. Neptune
I. Mercury

Go On ▶

Analysis: Choice G is correct. The order, from smallest to largest, of the bodies given is Pluto, Earth's Moon, Mercury, and Neptune.

Question **22** *assesses:*

Strand E: Earth and Space

Standard 1: The student understands the interaction and organization in the Solar System and the universe and how this affects life on Earth.

SC.E.1.3.4 The student knows that stars appear to be made of similar chemical elements, although they differ in age, size, temperature, and distance.

Student Strategies:

All stars in our universe are basically made of hydrogen that is fusing to become helium. However, stars can be different sizes, colors, temperatures, and ages. They often have different characteristics because of these differences.

The color of a star varies from red to blue, as the star becomes hotter. Our sun is a very average star in most respects. It is slightly above average in size. The smallest stars may be as small as 1/12th the size of our sun and the largest may be thousands of times as massive.

As a star ages, it burns through its hydrogen fuel and eventually collapses into a smaller form called a White Dwarf. If the star is more massive, it may explode into a supernova before collapsing into a neutron star. However, if a star is very massive, it may instead form a black hole after collapsing.

Many things can affect how a star appears from Earth. A star that looks smaller than another star may actually be larger, but farther away.

22 Our Sun is a yellow star. Stars can also be blue, blue-white, yellow-white, orange, or red. What does the star's color tell you about the star?

    A. exact size
    B. distance from Earth
    C. age in years
    D. temperature

Go On ▶

Analysis: Choice D is correct. The color of a star reflects its internal temperature. Choice C is incorrect because it is difficult to tell the exact age of a single star. Generally speaking, the color lets one know whether the star is early in its life cycle or near the end of its life, but the star's color is not an indicator of exact age. Choice B is incorrect because the distance from Earth varies among stars, but this is not reflected in the star's color. Choice A is only partly correct because although the color of a star lets you know how hot the star is burning, and how hot the star burns depends on its mass (i.e., the greater the star's mass, the hotter and faster it burns), color is not an indicator for the star's exact size.

Question **23** *assesses:*

Strand E: Earth and Space

Standard 2: The student recognizes the vastness of the universe and the Earth's place in it.

SC.E.2.3.1 The student knows that thousands of other galaxies appear to have the same elements, forces, and forms of energy found in our Solar System. [Also assesses: SC.E.1.3.3 The student understands that our sun is one of many stars in our galaxy.]

Student Strategies:

Our sun is the center of our solar system. Our solar system is one of billions, or even trillions, of stars in our Milky Way galaxy. A galaxy is a collection of stars that move as a group together. The universe is filled with millions of galaxies. These galaxies are held together by gravity.

Galaxies generally come in either spiral or elliptical form, although many galaxies are also irregularly shaped. Elliptical galaxies are generally very young, and become spiral-shaped as they get older. Many spiral galaxies also develop "arms" or bars of stars that extend from the center of the galaxy. Most of the stars in a galaxy are located in the center of the galaxy. Our sun is located along the edge of the Milky Way Galaxy.

Spiral Galaxy

Elliptical Galaxy

23 Galaxies come in a few specific shapes. Which of the following is not the name of a common galaxy shape?

F. spiral galaxy
G. cubital galaxy
H. elliptical galaxy
I. irregular galaxy

Go On ▶

Analysis: *Choice G is correct. Cubital is not a term used to describe galaxies. Choices F, H, and I are all common types of galaxies.*

Question **24** *assesses:*

Strand F: Processes of Life

Standard 1: The student describes patterns of structure and function in living things.

SC.F.1.3.1 The student understands that living things are composed of major systems that function in reproduction, growth, maintenance, and regulation.

Student Strategies:

The major body systems that help the body function include:

Skeletal system: The skeletal system is made up of bones that support the body and help it move.

Circulatory system: The circulatory system is made up of blood vessels that transport blood throughout the body. Blood provides nutrients to the body's cells and collects waste from them. The circulatory system is powered by the heart.

Muscular system: The muscular system is composed of muscles throughout the body. Muscles are responsible for moving the body, as well as providing the motion for other body organs, such as the heart and lungs, to function.

Digestive system: The digestive system takes in food and breaks it down into nutrients the body can absorb and use. Parts of the digestive system include the mouth, teeth, esophagus, stomach, liver, gallbladder, pancreas, small intestines, and large intestines.

Nervous system: The nervous system processes information about the environment and transmits information and commands throughout the body. The brain and spinal cord are the main components of the nervous system, along with the network of nerve cells that transmit information.

Respiratory system: The respiratory system takes in oxygen and releases carbon dioxide. Gas exchange takes place in the lungs.

Reproductive system: The reproductive system produces male and female gametes that combine to create a fetus for reproduction.

Go On ▶

24 In a normal adult, where are red blood cells produced?

A. in bones
B. in the dermis
C. in the plasma
D. in the atrium

Go On ▶

Analysis: *Choice A is correct. The major function of bone marrow is the production of red blood cells. Choice B is incorrect because the dermis is a part of the skin which has nothing to do with blood production. Choice C is incorrect because plasma is a part of the blood, but it is not involved in the production of any blood component. Choice D is incorrect because the atrium (a region within the heart) is involved in pumping blood, not producing it.*

Question **25** assesses:

Strand F: Processes of Life

Standard 1: The student describes patterns of structure and function in living things.

SC.F.1.3.2 The student knows that the structural basis of most organisms is the cell and most organisms are single cells, while some, including humans, are multicellular.

Student Strategies:

All living organisms are made up of one or more cells. Most of the organisms found on Earth are single-celled organisms, such as bacteria. However, many more complex organisms, such as animals and plants are made of many, even millions, of cells that work together.

In multicellular organisms, cells develop and become different from each other in order to do different jobs. For example, the cells that make up your muscles are very different from the cells that make up your bones.

Below are illustrations of the typical plant and animal cells that make up multicellular organisms.

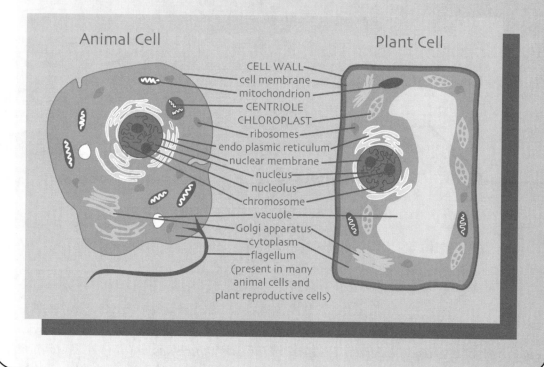

Copying is Prohibited
© Englefield & Associates, Inc.

25 Which of the following is **true** of both a bacterium and an eagle?

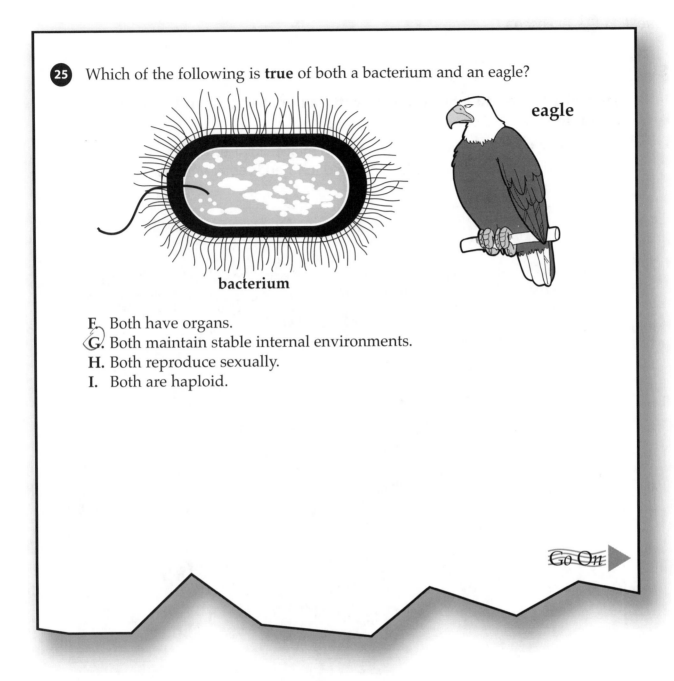

eagle

bacterium

F. Both have organs.
G. Both maintain stable internal environments.
H. Both reproduce sexually.
I. Both are haploid.

Go On ▶

Analysis: *Choice G is correct. Homeostasis (maintaining a stable internal environment) is a feature of all living things. Choice F is incorrect since organs are multi-cellular structures and cannot be present in the unicellular bacterium. Choice H is incorrect since bacteria reproduce asexually. Choice I is incorrect because eagles and all other vertebrates are diploid (containing two sets of chromosomes).*

Question **26** *assesses:*

Strand F: Processes of Life

Standard 1: The student describes patterns of structure and function in living things.

SC.F.1.3.3 The student knows that in multicellular organisms cells grow and divide to make more cells in order to form and repair various organs and tissues.

Student Strategies:

The cells of multicellular organisms go through stages called the cell cycle. The majority of time a cell is in interphase. In interphase the cell experiences growth and goes about the regular activities of life. Toward the end of interphase, the cell prepares to divide by making more DNA and creating the materials needed for division, or mitosis. The phases of mitosis are shown below:

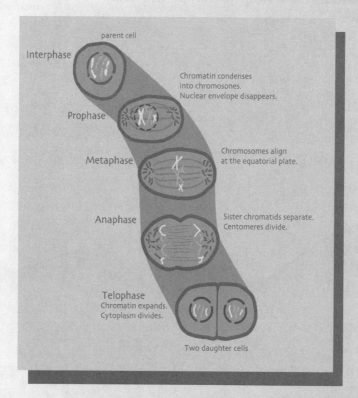

At the end of mitosis, the cell contains two nuclei with identical DNA. At this point the cell undergoes cytokinesis, the process in which the cell itself splits in two, with a nucleus in each new cell.

26 What are the products of mitosis?

A. four haploid cells
B. two cells that each have complimentary DNA
C. two new gametes
D. two new cells identical to each other

Go On ▶

Analysis: Choice D is correct. The purpose of mitosis is to create new cells that are identical to the original. Choice A is incorrect since four haploid cells are the product of meiosis. Choice B is incorrect because with mitosis the new cells have identical DNA, not complimentary DNA. Choice C is incorrect because gamete is the name for cells produced via meiosis.

Question **27** *assesses:*

Strand F: Processes of Life

Standard 1: The student describes patterns of structure and function in living things.

SC.F.1.3.4 The student knows that the levels of structural organization for function in living things include cells, tissues, organs, systems, and organisms.

Student Strategies:

Multicellular organisms are all made up of cells at the most basic level. However, similar types of cells can group and work together as tissues. Tissues can combine to work together as organs. Finally, different organs can combine to create organ systems.

Below is an illustration of how this organization works to create parts of the muscular and circulatory system. Heart muscle cells combine to create heart muscle tissue. The heart muscle tissue works together to function as a heart. The heart is the main organ in the circulatory system.

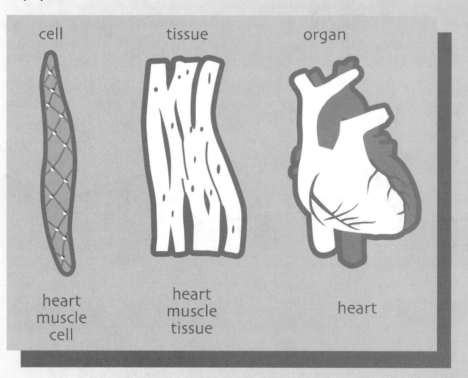

27 What is the direct result of more than one tissue working together to perform a specific function?

F. system
G. organ
H. operon
I. integument

Go On ▶

Analysis: *Choice G is correct. An organ is composed of at least two tissues. Choice F is incorrect. A system is a set of at least two organs. Choice H is incorrect because an operon is a unit of DNA. Choice I is incorrect because an integument is something that covers. For example, the integumentary system, which is more than just some tissues, protects the body.*

Question **28** *assesses:*

Strand F: Processes of Life

Standard 1: The student describes patterns of structure and function in living things.

SC.F.1.3.5 The student explains how the life functions of organisms are related to what occurs within the cell.

Student Strategies:

If you are asked about differences in cells in an organism, you can usually figure out the answer by reasoning. You know that cells in an organism become different, depending on what jobs they will be doing. Use your knowledge of the work the cell needs to do to figure out how the cell might differ. In reverse, if you are told the differences between some cells, try to imagine what types of jobs those cells might be better suited to perform.

For example, suppose a question asks you to think about differences in the cells of a plant's leaf compared to the cells in a plant's stem. You know that plant leaves are big and spongy. In contrast, a plant stem is tough and dense. Plant leaves are spread out in front of the sun to collect solar energy for photosynthesis. You can reason that they might be filled with chloroplasts and green pigment. Since they are spongy, you might guess that the cells might also be filled with water. In contrast, the cells that make up a plant's stem are thick and tough, with little or no chloroplasts. This is because a stem must function to hold the plant upright instead of collecting sunlight.

You can use this type of reasoning to answer questions about both plant, animal, or human cells.

28 A flower's cells can produce energy from light by the process of photosynthesis. If a flower is exposed to light from one direction, only the side of the flower that is exposed to the light will be able to produce energy. How will the plant respond?

    A. It will grow more slowly because of the lack of energy from the underexposed cells.

    B. It will grow more on the dark side, causing the plant to bend.

    C. It will grow more cells on the light side to increase the number of cells exposed to the light.

    D. It will grow more roots to increase the amount of energy taken from the soil.

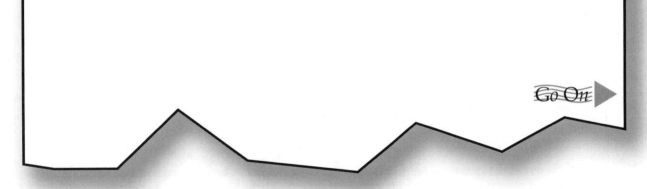

Go On ▶

Analysis: Choice B is correct. When one side of a plant is underexposed to light, that side will grow longer and cause the plant to bend, which will allow for more direct light exposure. Choice A is incorrect because growth will actually increase. Choice C is incorrect because more growth occurs on the dark side, not the light side. Choice D is incorrect because energy is not taken in from the soil.

Question **29** *assesses:*

Strand F: Processes of Life

Standard 1: The student describes patterns of structure and function in living things.

SC.F.1.3.6 The student knows that the cells with similar functions have similar structures, whereas those with different structures have different functions.

Student Strategies:

When you must answer a question about cells with different structures or functions, start by making a table comparing and contrasting the differences in the cells. For example, nerve cells are long and stringy. This is because they serve to transport information throughout the cells of the body. Nerve cells are like telephone wires in both function and form. In contrast, fat cells are big and round, with much more flexibility in movement and growth potential. This is because fat cells are used to store food and energy for an organism.

If you are asked about a type of cell or function that you are unfamiliar with, list the properties that you think might be helpful for a cell to carry out the needed functions. Often you can determine the answer through deduction.

29 Sickle-cell disease is a condition in which red blood cells have a protein that changes the shape of the cell. Why is this condition dangerous?

F. The new shape hinders the cell's function.
G. The protein that controls the cell's shape also stops the cell from reproducing.
H. A cell cannot survive if it changes shape.
I. A red blood cell will no longer be a red blood cell if it changes shape.

Go On ▶

Analysis: *Choice F is correct. The round shape of normal red blood cells allows for efficient transport of oxygen. Choice G is incorrect because individual blood cells do not replicate. Choice H is incorrect because the cells can survive, they just cannot efficiently transport oxygen. Choice I is incorrect because the definition of a red blood cell is not based on its shape.*

Question **30** *assesses:*

Strand F: Processes of Life

Standard 1: The student describes patterns of structure and function in living things.

SC.F.1.3.7 The student knows that behavior is a response to the environment and influences growth, development, maintenance, and reproduction.

Student Strategies:

Behavior is a response that an organism has to its environment. All organisms respond with behavior that maintains stability for themselves. Organisms evolve and develop behavior that helps them survive environmental changes and reproduce. Organisms that are unable to change or respond to changes in their environment are less successful in reproducing and may even die.

Behaviors can either be instinctive, or learned. For example, spiders know how to create intricate webs without being taught. This behavior is instinctive, or innate. On the other hand, many animals must learn how to hunt or obtain food by watching their parents. This behavior is learned.

30 Plants absorb water into their roots from the soil. Plants also release water into the atmosphere through structures call stomata on the leaves. What happens to the plant if there is **more** water leaving through the stomata than there is entering through the roots?

  A. The plant will bend toward the angle of the sunlight.
  B. The plant will not be affected.
  C. The plant will lose rigidity and wilt.
  D. The plant will increase its rate of growth.

Go On ▶

Analysis: Choice C is correct. Water contributes to the plant's rigidity. If more water is leaving the plant than is entering it, the plant will lose its rigidity. Choice A is incorrect because this refers to the process of phototropism, which is related to light, not water. Choice B is incorrect because the plant will be affected. Choice D is incorrect because the rate of growth will not increase with water loss.

Question **31** *assesses:*

Strand F: Processes of Life

Standard 2: The student understands the process and importance of genetic diversity.

SC.F.2.3.1 The student knows the patterns and advantages of sexual and asexual reproduction in plants and animals.

Student Strategies:

You should be familiar with the processes of sexual and asexual reproduction in organisms. Each of these reproductive processes has advantages and disadvantages. Both processes have the same goal: to reproduce and allow the species to survive.

Asexual

- Usually favored by one-celled organisms, such as bacteria

- Requires only one parent

- Results in a new organism with the exact genetic makeup as the parent

- Can happen quickly and efficiently

Sexual

- Usually favored by larger, multi-cellular organisms

- Requires two or more parents

- Results in a new organism with a mixture of genetic material from parents

- Often slower and may use a lot of the parents' resources

- Increases genetic diversity

Copying is Prohibited
© Englefield & Associates, Inc.

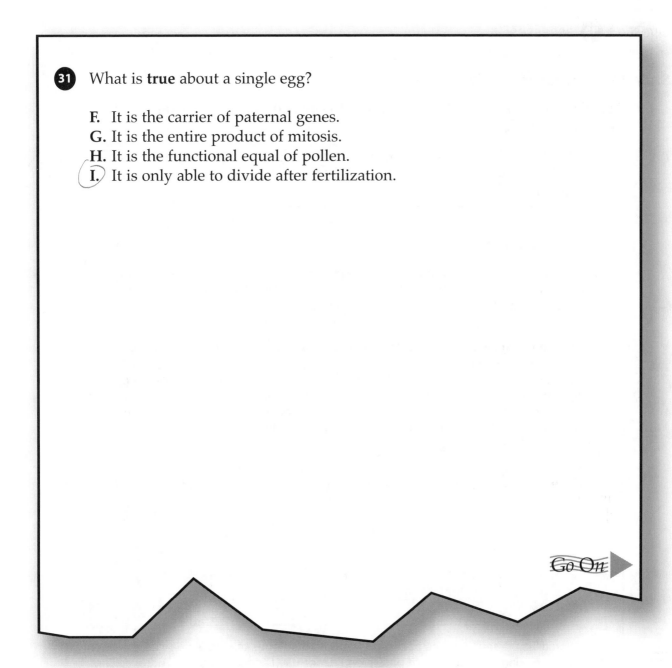

31 What is **true** about a single egg?

    F. It is the carrier of paternal genes.
    G. It is the entire product of mitosis.
    H. It is the functional equal of pollen.
    I. It is only able to divide after fertilization.

Go On ▶

Analysis: *Choice I is correct. An egg is inactive until after fertilization. Choice F is incorrect because eggs are produced by females and, therefore, carry the maternal genes. Choice G is incorrect because eggs are produced by meiosis. Choice H is incorrect because pollen is the male gamete in plants, not the female.*

Question **32** *assesses:*

Strand F: Processes of Life

Standard 2: The student understands the process and importance of genetic diversity.

SC.F.2.3.2 The student knows that the variation in each species is due to the exchange and interaction of genetic information as it is passed from parent to offspring.

Student Strategies:

Sexual reproduction creates new combinations of traits in offspring because each parent contributes different genes that are passed on. You should be familiar with Punnett squares, and how they work. You may need to fill out a Punnett square in order to answer questions about how genes are passed on to offspring from parents.

You should first know whether a gene is dominant or recessive. Dominant genes express themselves even if there is only one dominant gene present. They are usually indicated by a capital letter. For example, if B represents the gene that gives a dog brown fur, then a dog with one dominant and one recessive gene would be designated by Bb and would have brown hair. A BB dog would have both dominant genes and be brown, while a bb dog would have only recessive genes and would not be brown.

You can fill out a Punnett square to determine the probability of different genes being passed on to offspring. If you had a dog with brown fur that had both dominant genes mate with a dog with white fur that had both recessive genes, you might make a table like this:

		Dominant brown-fur dog	
		B	B
Recessive white-fur dog	b		
	b		

You then fill in the four squares between them with the genes that would be passed on. In this case, the dominant dog would pass along either one B gene or another B gene. The recessive dog would pass on one b gene or another b gene.

		Dominant brown-fur dog	
		B	B
Recessive white-fur dog	b	Bb	Bb
	b	Bb	Bb

In this case, all offspring would be Bb, with brown fur.

32 If two people who are both heterozygous for eye color (Pp) mate, how many possible genotypes are there for the offspring?

    A. 1
    B. 2
    C. 3
    D. 4

Go On ▶

Analysis: Choice C is correct. Heterozygous means having two different alleles in the gene pair; one is dominant (P) and one is recessive (p). The possible offspring are PP, Pp, and pp.

Question **33** *assesses:*

Strand F: Processes of Life

Standard 2: The student understands the process and importance of genetic diversity.

SC.F.2.3.3 The student knows that generally organisms in a population live long enough to reproduce because they have survival characteristics.

Student Strategies:

The ultimate goal for behavior or characteristics of an organism or species is to survive and reproduce. When you must evaluate a characteristic or change, try to think about how that change might help or hurt an organism's ability to survive or create offspring.

Over many generations, characteristics or behaviors that help an organism survive will typically become more common. Characteristics that hurt an organism's chances of surviving or reproducing will eventually disappear as organisms with these characteristics do not survive long enough to reproduce. Most new characteristics or behaviors begin as random events. It is only after several generations of reproduction that some of these traits become more common as they have caused individuals that have the traits to be more successful than other organisms.

33 Rabbits that live in snow in the arctic are almost always white. Why are the non-white rabbits in this region **less** likely to pass on their fur color to offspring?

    F. Non-white rabbits are easy to see in the snow and more likely to be eaten before they are able to mate.

    G. White rabbits are already more numerous, so it is too difficult for the non-white rabbits to pass on their color.

    H. The white rabbits will be more effective hunters and, therefore, more healthy.

    I. The white rabbits choose not to mate with the non-white rabbits.

Go On ▶

Analysis: Choice F is correct. Non-white rabbits will be obvious to predators and are less likely to survive to mating age. Choice G is incorrect because the number of white rabbits would not affect the ability to pass on the non-white color. The non-white rabbits would simply have to find another rabbit (white or otherwise) with which to mate. Choice H is incorrect because rabbits are not hunters. Choice I is incorrect because fur color is not a factor in mate choice.

Question **34** *assesses:*

Strand F: Processes of Life

> **Standard 2: The student understands the process and importance of genetic diversity.**
>
> > **SC.F.2.3.4** The student knows that the fossil record provides evidence that changes in the kinds of plants and animals in the environment have been occurring over time.

Student Strategies:

Fossils are created when organisms die and their bodies are preserved in rock, mud, or other medium that hardens and survives over thousands or even millions of years. Although the occurrence of fossils varies throughout history, there are still many organisms from long ago that scientists can study today because they became fossils.

Fossils can be dated several different ways. Fossils, like rocks, are generally deposited in the soil in horizontal layers. So fossils nearer the surface are usually younger than fossils deeper down. Also, fossils are the same age as the rocks they are found in or around, so if the ages of the rocks around them can be determined, so can the age of the fossil.

Go On

34 Which of the following is **most** useful when trying to figure out how plants and animals have changed over time?

   A. fossils
   B. soil
   C. knowledge of plants' and animals' life spans
   D. knowledge of plants' and animals' reproductive processes

Go On ▶

Analysis: Choice A is correct. Fossils provide a historical context in which it is possible to determine change. Choice B is incorrect because soil does not provide any of this type of information. Choices C and D both provide some understanding and can be useful in the context provided by fossils, but these things do not provide much information about change by themselves.

Question **35** *assesses:*

Strand G: How Living Things Interact with Their Environment

> **Standard 1: The student understands the competitive, interdependent, cyclic nature of living things in the environment.**
>
> > **SC.G.1.3.2** The student knows that biological adaptations include changes in structures, behaviors, or physiology that enhance reproductive success in a particular environment.

Student Strategies:

Although the new physical characteristics or behaviors that organisms exhibit are usually random in origin, they may be either helpful or harmful to the organism's ability to survive and reproduce. If the adaptation is helpful, it will increase in occurrence because it will allow those organisms to live and reproduce, passing on their characteristics to new offspring.

The new characteristics that develop can be either a change in a specific structure of an organism, such as a change in a bird's beak, or an animal's claw, or the change can also take the form of a behavior, such as a mating ritual or nesting ability. It may take the form of a difference in physiology, or body type.

When thinking about whether a change is adaptive (helpful) or non-adaptive (harmful), it is wise to consider the organism's environment. Most organisms develop specific characteristics or behaviors that help them adapt to a specific environment, or niche. By becoming better at surviving in this specific environment, they are able to out-compete other organisms' lack of special skills or structures. Specialization can make them successful in their environment. For example, polar bears are white. Since they live in snowy environments, their white fur helps them hide from potential prey.

35 The rattlesnake shown below matches the color of the desert environment in which it lives. This makes it easier for the snake to hunt prey and avoid predators.

Which of the following describes the snake's coloring?

F. modification
G. adaptation
H. formation
I. speciation

Analysis: Choice G is correct. The snake's color makes it adapted for its specific environment. Choice F is incorrect because a modification is simply a change, not necessarily a change for a specific environment. Choice H is incorrect because the color is not a new feature being formed; it is simply a change in a pre-existing feature (namely skin color). Choice I is incorrect because speciation is the formation of a new species, which is not occurring here.

Question **36** *assesses:*

Strand G: How Living Things Interact with Their Environment

> **Standard 1: The student understands the competitive, interdependent, cyclic nature of living things in the environment.**

>> **SC.G.1.3.3** The student understands that the classification of living things is based on a given set of criteria and is a tool for understanding biodiversity and interrelationships.

Student Strategies:

Scientists classify organisms according to their characteristics. Organisms are classified into Kingdoms, Phylum, Classes, Orders, Family, Genus and Species. This classification goes from general to most specific. The more classification levels that two organisms have in common, the more closely they are related and the more similar they are to each other. For example, although snails and elephants are both in the Animal Kingdom, they are not as closely related as two different species of birds.

Scientists who work on classification are known as taxonomists. They examine many different characteristics when classifying organisms. These characteristics include, size, shape, movement, growth, and reproduction. In addition, scientists often compare the DNA of different organisms to see how similar they are for classification purposes.

36 A genus is a group of species. When a scientist discovers a new species, how does he or she know in which genus it should be placed?

   A. The new species is placed with the species it was discovered with.
   B. A new genus is created for new species.
   C. The new species is placed with the species with which it shares the most characteristics.
   D. The new species is placed with species from a similar geographic region.

Go On ▶

Analysis: *Choice C is correct. A genus is a group of closely related species, and species is determined by similarity. Choice A is incorrect because new species are often discovered with completely unrelated species and such a grouping would be meaningless. Choice B is incorrect because it would mean that every species would have its own genus. Choice D is incorrect because many different types of organisms can live in the same area even if they are not closely related.*

Question **37** *assesses:*

Strand G: How Living Things Interact with Their Environment

Standard 1: The student understands the competitive, interdependent, cyclic nature of living things in the environment.

SC.G.1.3.4 The student knows that the interactions of organisms with each other and with the nonliving parts of their environments result in the flow of energy and the cycling of matter throughout the system. [Also assesses: SC.G.1.3.1 The student knows that viruses depend on other living things. SC.G.1.3.5 The student knows that life is maintained by a continuous input of energy from the sun and by the recycling of the atoms that make up the molecules of living organisms.]

Student Strategies:

Energy travels through organisms in a food chain. As energy moves from one level to the next, some energy is lost as waste heat.

Producers are organisms that convert energy from sunlight into sugars that can be used by themselves and by other organisms.

Consumers are other organisms that obtain energy from producers or other consumers. Herbivores are organisms that obtain energy directly from eating plants. Carnivores are organisms that obtain energy indirectly from plants by eating other organisms that have eaten plants. Omnivores are organisms that eat plants and animals.

Herbivores are also known as primary consumers. Carnivores are also known as secondary consumers. Carnivores that eat other carnivores may be known as tertiary, or higher, consumers.

Decomposers are organisms such as bacteria or fungi that break down dead organisms into basic components.

37 READ INQUIRE EXPLAIN　　Go to your Science Practice Tutorial Answer Sheet to answer Number 37.

Go On ▶

Analysis: Organisms that obtain food directly from the Sun are producers, or plants. During photosynthesis, green plants use energy that is taken in from the Sun to convert water, carbon dioxide, and minerals into oxygen and other compounds.

Question **38** *assesses:*

Strand G: How Living Things Interact with Their Environment

Standard 2: The student understands the consequences of using limited natural resources.

SC.B.2.3.1 The student knows that some resources are renewable and others are nonrenewable. [Also assesses: SC.B.2.3.2 The student knows that most of the energy used today is derived from burning stored energy collected by organisms millions of years ago (i.e., nonrenewable fossil fuels).]

Student Strategies:

Energy is obtained from either renewable or nonrenewable resources. A renewable resource is one that does not run out. Some renewable resources include solar energy, wind power, nuclear energy, hydroelectric power, and geothermal energy. Although renewable energy sources provide an endless supply of energy, they have drawbacks. Some renewable energy resources release pollution, while others are costly or less efficient that nonrenewable resources.

Most of the energy used by society right now comes from nonrenewable sources. Humans rely mostly on fossil fuels, such as oil, coal, and natural gas. Fossil fuels come from living organisms that died millions of years ago whose remains have changed with time and pressure. Although using fossil fuels is fairly cheap, they release large amounts of carbon dioxide and other pollutants into the air. Since supplies of nonrenewable resources are limited, it is important for humans to find other sources of energy to replace them when they are gone.

38 Which of the following is a nonrenewable resource?

F. wind
G. coal
H. plants
I. water

Go On ▶

Analysis: Choice G is correct. Coal is the only resource above that is limited. Choices F, H, and I can all be replenished, which makes them incorrect.

Question **39** *assesses:*

Strand G: How Living Things Interact with Their Environment

Standard 2: The student understands the consequences of using limited natural resources.

SC.G.2.3.2 The student knows that all biotic and abiotic factors are interrelated and that if one factor is changed or removed, it impacts the availability of other resources within the system.

Student Strategies:

An environment can be divided into biotic and abiotic factors. Biotic factors are the living things in that environment. Abiotic factors are the non-living things in the environment. Both biotic and abiotic factors affect an organism's ability to survive and reproduce in the environment. Biotic and abiotic factors are linked as well. Changes that occur in one type of environmental factor affect the other factors.

Some examples of abiotic factors include the amount of light, the type of air, the temperature, the pH level, the water available, the type of soil, and the pollution present in the environment.

Some examples of biotic factors include the food or prey organisms, predators, organisms that compete for resources, and pathogens.

39 Which of the following things shown in the pond ecosystem below is an abiotic feature?

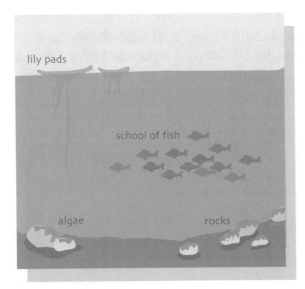

lily pads

school of fish

algae   rocks

  A. a school of small fish
  B. lily pads on the pond's surface
  C. rocks at the bottom of the pond
  D. algae on the rocks at the bottom of the pond

Go On ▶

Analysis: Choice C is correct. An abiotic feature is a non-living component of the ecosystem. Choices A, B, and D are all living and, therefore, are incorrect.

Question **40** *assesses:*

Strand G: How Living Things Interact with Their Environment

Standard 2: The student understands the consequences of using limited natural resources.

SC.G.2.3.3 The student knows that a brief change in the limited resources of an ecosystem may alter the size of a population or the average size of individual organisms and that long-term change may result in the elimination of animal and plant populations inhabiting the Earth.

Student Strategies:

When considering how a change in resources affects the population of a species, try to think about how the organisms of that species utilize the resource. An increase in availability of vital resources, such as food, living space, or water will typically allow a population to grow. However, keep in mind that as a population grows, it also requires more resources to sustain that population level. In addition, the increase in a population also means that more waste will be produced by the organisms.

Think about the other ways that an increase in population can affect an environment. As a population changes, it affects the biotic factors in the environment as well. For example, as a population increases, it consumes other organisms, and uses more resources, causing a decline in other populations. A meadow that experiences a dramatic increase in rabbit population will eventually experience a decline in the amount of clover plants. If the rabbit population continues to grow, the clover plants may disappear completely from the meadow.

40 Which of the following abiotic features is **most** important in determining the number of plants that can survive in a given environment on Earth?

F. rainfall
G. predators
H. wind direction
I. soil depth

Go On ▶

Analysis: *Choice F is correct. Choice G, predators, is a biotic factor, since it describes a living component. Choices H and I affect which types of plants can survive in an environment. Rainfall, and therefore water, is the only choice that is a limiting abiotic resource.*

Question **41** *assesses:*

Strand G: How Living Things Interact with Their Environment

Standard 2: The student understands the consequences of using limited natural resources.

SC.G.2.3.4 The student understands that humans are a part of an ecosystem and their activities may deliberately or inadvertently alter the equilibrium in ecosystems. [Also assesses: SC.D.2.3.2 The student knows the positive and negative consequences of human action on the Earth's systems.]

Student Strategies:

You should be aware of how human activity affects the environment. As the human population has multiplied in the last several hundred years, our impact on the planet has increased dramatically.

Humans' impact on the planet takes two basic forms. First, as humans become more numerous, we use more of Earth's resources. Second, we release more of our waste into the environment.

When you evaluate human activity on the environment, remember that resources take many different forms. We use more plants and animals for food, cut down more trees for building supplies, and burn more fossil fuels for energy. We also use more oxygen, clean water, and living space. Using these resources means there are less resources available for other animals and plants. We also damage the air, water, and biotic environment as well.

Some common environmental problems caused by humans, include acid rain, global warming, and the depletion of the ozone layer. As humans need more and more resources, we destroy forest areas and water sources that other plants and animals must use to survive. Human activity is the leading cause of species extinctions right now.

41 If pollution caused the overall temperature on Earth to increase by a few degrees, what would be the **most** dangerous effect?

　　A. an increased risk of heat stroke
　　B. melting of the polar ice caps
　　C. more rainfall in the tropics
　　D. a decrease of carbon dioxide available to plants

Go On ▶

Analysis: Choice B is correct. Global warming would melt the ice caps and lead to coastal flooding. Choice A is incorrect because heat stroke would not be caused by only a few degrees change. Choice C is incorrect because, although rainfall may be increased, it would not be notably dangerous. Choice D is incorrect because carbon dioxide levels are positively tied to temperature, so there is no reason carbon dioxide levels would decrease as temperature increases.

Question **42** *assesses:*

Strand H: The Nature of Science

> **Standard 1: The student uses the scientific processes and habits of mind to solve problems.**
>
>> **SC.H.1.3.1** The student knows that scientific knowledge is subject to modification as new information challenges prevailing theories and as a new theory leads to looking at old observations in a new way.

Student Strategies:

Science is not just a list of facts and laws. Science is always in motion. One of the principles of scientific study is that knowledge is available to all people and any scientific study is open to criticism or testing by other scientists.

No scientific knowledge provides the whole "truth." Instead, knowledge is tested and added to what scientists have learned in the past. This is why the efforts of scientists that made observations hundreds and even thousands of years ago are still very important. When a scientist makes a discovery, it is usually termed that he or she is "standing on the shoulders of giants." This means that the scientist could not have made this discovery without using the knowledge gained by many scientists in the past.

Another way that past scientific knowledge is important is because it allows new scientists to look at older studies and knowledge with fresh perspective. Many scientific discoveries are made by scientists who study older scientific theories and then offer new ideas.

42 Scientists today are conducting research to answer questions that were considered unanswerable 100 years ago. Why are modern scientists able to examine things that past scientists were **not** able to explore?

    F. People today are smarter than people were in the past.
    G. Scientists today are able to use past research to expand their current understanding.
    H. As time passes, certain facts become easier to understand.
    I. Science repeats itself over time.

Go On ▶

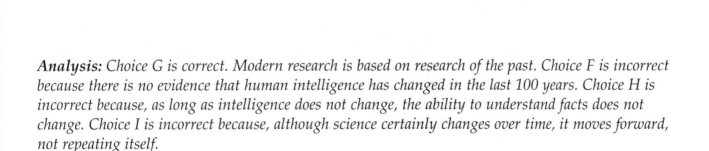

Analysis: Choice G is correct. Modern research is based on research of the past. Choice F is incorrect because there is no evidence that human intelligence has changed in the last 100 years. Choice H is incorrect because, as long as intelligence does not change, the ability to understand facts does not change. Choice I is incorrect because, although science certainly changes over time, it moves forward, not repeating itself.

Question **43** *assesses:*

Strand H: The Nature of Science

Standard 1: The student uses the scientific processes and habits of mind to solve problems.

SC.H.1.3.2 The student knows that the study of the events that led scientists to discoveries can provide information about the inquiry process and its effects.

Student Strategies:

Scientists use an ordered series of steps when conducting an investigation. These steps are called scientific methods. The scientific methods that scientists use are:

1. Make observations about something and ask questions about what has been observed.

2. Develop a hypothesis about why something happens. A hypothesis is an explanation that can be tested through an experiment or set of observations.

3. Plan an investigation or series of observations that will test the hypothesis.

4. Conduct the investigation or observations.

5. Collect results of the investigation or observations. Evaluate any data and reach a conclusion based on the results.

6. Write up a report that describes the investigation and results.

43 You are conducting an experiment to examine how the size of a flower is affected by some of the conditions in which the flower grows. Which of the following should you do **first**?

A. measure the size of the growing flowers
B. create a hypothesis
C. evaluate collected data
D. determine the variable to be tested

Go On ▶

Analysis: Choice D is correct. The first step in scientific inquiry is to determine exactly what will be tested. Choice A is incorrect because data collection cannot occur until after the experiment is well underway. Choice B is incorrect because a hypothesis cannot be created until the question to be addressed has been formulated. Choice C is incorrect because data evaluation is one of the last steps of scientific inquiry.

Question **44** *assesses:*

Strand H: The Nature of Science

> **Standard 1: The student uses the scientific processes and habits of mind to solve problems.**
>
> > **SC.H.1.3.3** The student knows that science disciplines differ from one another in topic, techniques, and outcomes, but that they share a common purpose, philosophy, and enterprise.

Student Strategies:

Although science has many different branches and disciplines, all scientists go about learning the same way. All scientists use scientific methods to make discoveries. In addition, all scientists publish their investigations and results so that other scientists can question and repeat their studies. No matter what a scientist studies, he or she strives to avoid bias and conduct an investigation that leads to useful knowledge.

Because scientists have the same methods and goals, they can often collaborate together to conduct important investigations. For example, if scientists wished to learn more about bacteria in volcanic vents, a geologist who knows about volcanoes might team up with a microbiologist who studies bacteria. Often scientists are able to make important discoveries by combining their different backgrounds for a common cause.

Go On

44 In chemistry, objects as small as a single atom are studied. In astronomy, objects as large as entire solar systems and galaxies are studied. Why is it that, although they study such drastically different objects, both fields are considered science?

F. They both use the same technology.
G. They both require the same basic knowledge.
H. They both use the same basic scientific methods.
I. They are both based on the same original experiments.

Go On ▶

Analysis: *Choice H is correct. All science is based on the same basic methods. Choice F is incorrect because these different fields use very different technologies. Choice G is incorrect because science is defined by a process, not by the facts involved. Choice I is incorrect because there are no such experiments.*

Question **45** *assesses:*

Strand H: The Nature of Science

> **Standard 1: The student uses the scientific processes and habits of mind to solve problems.**
>
>> **SC.H.1.3.4** The student knows that accurate record keeping, openness, and replication are essential to maintaining an investigator's credibility with other scientists and society. [Also assesses: SC.H.1.3.7 The student knows that when similar investigations give different results, the scientific challenge is to verify whether the differences are significant by further study.]

Student Strategies:

It is important for all scientists to keep honest records of their investigations and to report their findings. Scientists must provide all of the data they collected, even if it does not support their hypothesis.

It is also important for other scientists to review the investigation and make criticisms. For this reason, a scientific investigation is not considered valid until it has been published in a reputable science magazine. At that point, other scientists can determine if the investigation was conducted correctly and if the data was interpreted in a fair way. Other scientists may also conduct the investigation for themselves to see if they get similar results.

Scientists who do not keep good records or are not honest about data are not conducting good science. Their results cannot be trusted, and may create confusion or errors.

Go On

45 When conducting experiments to attempt to find treatments for the West Nile Virus, a scientist does **not** keep accurate notes. What problem will this cause?

   A. It will be difficult to repeat and validate the results.
   B. It will be difficult to understand the conclusion.
   C. It will be difficult to understand the hypothesis.
   D. It will be difficult to understand how the treatment can be used.

Go On ▶

Analysis: Choice A is correct. Accurate notes allow an experiment to be repeated, which is necessary for validation. Choices B and C are incorrect because the notes are most important for the process of the experiment, not for the hypothesis or the conclusion. Choice D is incorrect because the ability to use the treatment would be something considered only after the experiment had been validated.

Question **46** *assesses:*

Strand H: The Nature of Science

> **Standard 1: The student uses the scientific processes and habits of mind to solve problems.**
>
> > **SC.H.1.3.5** The student knows that a change in one or more variables may alter the outcome of an investigation.

Student Strategies:

Scientists use controlled experiments to test ideas and hypotheses. A controlled experiment seeks to keep all factors, or variables, the same except for the factor that is being tested. All the parts of the experiment that must stay constant are called controlled variables. If controlled variables are allowed to change, the results of the experiment may not be valid.

The independent variable is the factor that the scientist changes in order to test the hypothesis. For example, if a scientist wants to test whether a certain type of fuel releases less air pollution in a car, the fuel type is the independent variable. To test this, the scientist needs to control the other variables, such as the type of car, the amount of fuel used, etc.

The dependent variable is the factor that is measured by the scientist. In the example above, the amount of air pollution released by the cars using different fuels is the dependent variable.

46 In biology class, you conduct an experiment to determine how plants grow in different types of soil. You have five types of soil and you plant four seeds from the same plant in each soil type. Each plant is kept in a room so that each has the same temperature, humidity, amount of water, and amount of sunlight. You then measure the heights of the plants after two weeks.

What is the independent variable in your experiment?

F. plant height
G. number of plants
H. soil type
I. amount of sunlight

Analysis: Choice H is correct. An independent variable is one that is manipulated by the experimenter. Choice F is incorrect because plant height is the dependent variable (one that responds to the independent variable). Choices G and I are incorrect because they are consistent for all samples.

Question **47** *assesses:*

Strand H: The Nature of Science

Standard 2: The student understands that most natural events occur in comprehensible, consistent patterns.

SC.H.2.3.1 The student recognizes that patterns exist within and across systems.

Student Strategies:

Scientific exploration is often about analyzing patterns. Scientists can often learn much about something by finding a pattern and using it to help explain or predict other events.

An example is in genetics. Scientists have discovered that all living things use DNA as a blueprint for their structures and processes. The pattern and processes of DNA is similar for all living organisms. Scientists are able to use information about DNA from organisms they've studied and apply that knowledge to other organisms they haven't studied.

You can use the process of pattern recognition as well. Try to think about the information you know and the information that is given to you. Look for any patterns and use these patterns to answer questions when you can. Having some knowledge about one system or type of system can often help you answer questions about a different system if you can apply a pattern.

47 The most common element in living organisms is carbon. As new plants and animals grow, a great deal of carbon is required. Where does **most** of Earth's available carbon come from?

    A. New carbon molecules are constantly being constructed from inorganic compounds.

    B. Carbon is cycled back into Earth's system from dead organisms.

    C. Carbon enters Earth's system with the energy from the Sun.

    D. There is an enormous amount of carbon that has been stored in Earth's soil.

Go On ▶

Analysis: Choice B is correct. Carbon cycles through living organisms when decomposers return the carbon from dead organisms to the ecosystems and it is consumed by another living organism. Choice A is incorrect because the amount of carbon on Earth is fixed; new carbon is not "created." Choice C is incorrect because energy is provided by the Sun; matter is not. Choice D is incorrect because carbon is usually in constant motion through the system.

Question **48** *assesses:*

Strand H: The Nature of Science

Standard 2: The student understands that most natural events occur in comprehensible, consistent patterns.

SC.H.3.3.1 The student knows that science ethics demand that scientists must not knowingly subject coworkers, students, the neighborhood, or the community to health or property risks. [Also assesses: SC.H.3.3.2 The student knows that special care must be taken in using animals in scientific research. SC.H.3.3.3 The student knows that in research involving human subjects, the ethics of science require that potential subjects be fully informed about the risks and benefits associated with the research and of their right to refuse to participate.]

Student Strategies:

Investigations often involve using humans or animals as test subjects. It is essential that scientists take great care to protect the health and safety of every living thing associated with the investigation.

This must be done in several ways. First, the scientist must make sure that safety procedures are being followed in the laboratory or investigation. In this way, the safety of everyone involved is protected. Secondly, when creating a procedure for an investigation, the safety of test subjects must be considered. Sometimes a procedure that might give better information must be discarded in favor of a less-effective procedure that better safeguards people or animals. Scientists must take special care in using animals, since they must be treated humanely, and cannot give informed consent.

Finally, the scientist must be sure to inform all humans involved in an investigation of the risks they will be taking. Any people taking part in an investigation should be completely aware of what will happen and how it could affect them. Only after all humans have been fully informed and have agreed to participate is it OK for a scientist to include them in a study.

48 There are many scientists and researchers currently working on medications and treatments for all types of medical ailments, from the common cold to deadly cancers. The government requires a great deal of research before allowing a medication to be sold to the public. Why is so much work required before medication can be made available?

    F. It is easier for the public if there are few medications to choose from.
    G. More research may find more uses for the new medication.
    H. All possible dangerous side effects must be examined.
    I. It must be shown that new medications are different from old ones.

Go On ▶

Analysis: Choice H is correct. The Food and Drug Administration (FDA) ensures, among other things, that new medications are safe for the public. Choice F is incorrect because the FDA does not concern itself with the total number of medical options. Choice G is incorrect because medications can be released, as long as they are safe, before new uses are researched. Choice I is incorrect because many medications are very similar to other medications.

Question **49** *assesses:*

Strand H: The Nature of Science

Standard 2: The student understands that most natural events occur in comprehensible, consistent patterns.

SC.H.3.3.4 The student knows that technological design should require taking into account constraints such as natural laws, the properties of the materials used, and economic, political, social, ethical, and aesthetic values. [Also assesses: SC.H.3.3.6 The student knows that no matter who does science and mathematics or invents things, or when or where they do it, the knowledge and technology that result can eventually become available to everyone. SC.H.3.3.37 The student knows that computers speed up and extend people's ability to collect, sort, and analyze data; prepare research reports; and share data and ideas with others.]

Student Strategies:

When considering a question that asks you to assess the impact of a type of technology, you should consider several things. Although technology primarily deals with overcoming physical or financial limitations, the social impact should also be considered.

Keep in mind that new technology must a) improve the ability to collect or analyze information, b) be cheap enough and easy enough to use, c) be legally acceptable, and d) be acceptable by social standards.

Scientific knowledge is for everyone. As such, it must be usable and acceptable to society at large. Important tools, such as microscopes, telescopes, computers, and other innovations meet all the requirements above and have become valuable resources. You can use these guides to evaluate other scientific tools or technologies.

49 Which of the following technologies has **most** affected the ability of astronomers to analyze information about our galaxy, the Milky Way?

A. telescopes
B. microscopes
C. refractive mirrors
D. computers

Go On ▶

Analysis: Choice D is correct. Computers have changed the way in which many types of scientists, including astronomers, can analyze data. Choices A and C are incorrect because they are involved in collecting astronomical data, not analyzing it. Choice B is incorrect because microscopes are rarely used in astronomy.

This is the end of the Science Practice Tutorial.
Until time is called, go back and check your work or answer questions you did not complete. When you have finished, close your workbook.

Answer Sheet

Name_____

Practice Tutorial Answer Sheet

Answer all the questions that appear in the Practice Tutorial on this Answer Sheet. Answer multiple-choice questions by filling in the bubble for the answer you select. Answer gridded-response questions by filling in the correct bubbles. Write your answers to "Read, Inquire, Explain" questions on the lines provided.

To remove your Answer Sheet, carefully tear along the dotted line.

1. Ⓐ Ⓑ Ⓒ Ⓓ   2. Ⓕ Ⓖ Ⓗ Ⓘ   3. Ⓐ Ⓑ Ⓒ Ⓓ

4. Ⓕ Ⓖ Ⓗ Ⓘ   5. Ⓐ Ⓑ Ⓒ Ⓓ   6. Ⓕ Ⓖ Ⓗ Ⓘ

7. Ⓐ Ⓑ Ⓒ Ⓓ   8. Ⓕ Ⓖ Ⓗ Ⓘ   9. Ⓐ Ⓑ Ⓒ Ⓓ

10. Ⓕ Ⓖ Ⓗ Ⓘ   11. Ⓐ Ⓑ Ⓒ Ⓓ   12. Ⓕ Ⓖ Ⓗ Ⓘ

13. Ⓐ Ⓑ Ⓒ Ⓓ   14. Ⓕ Ⓖ Ⓗ Ⓘ   15.

	/	/	/	
•	•	•	•	•
0	0	0	0	0
1	1	1	1	1
2	2	2	2	2
3	3	3	3	3
4	4	4	4	4
5	5	5	5	5
6	6	6	6	6
7	7	7	7	7
8	8	8	8	8
9	9	9	9	9

16. Ⓐ Ⓑ Ⓒ Ⓓ   17. Ⓕ Ⓖ Ⓗ Ⓘ   18. Ⓐ Ⓑ Ⓒ Ⓓ

Fold and Tear Carefully Along Dotted Line.

Go On ▶

19　Ⓕ　Ⓖ　Ⓗ　Ⓘ　　　20　Ⓐ　Ⓑ　Ⓒ　Ⓓ　　　21　Ⓕ　Ⓖ　Ⓗ　Ⓘ

22　Ⓐ　Ⓑ　Ⓒ　Ⓓ　　　23　Ⓕ　Ⓖ　Ⓗ　Ⓘ　　　24　Ⓐ　Ⓑ　Ⓒ　Ⓓ

25　Ⓕ　Ⓖ　Ⓗ　Ⓘ　　　26　Ⓐ　Ⓑ　Ⓒ　Ⓓ　　　27　Ⓕ　Ⓖ　Ⓗ　Ⓘ

28　Ⓐ　Ⓑ　Ⓒ　Ⓓ　　　29　Ⓕ　Ⓖ　Ⓗ　Ⓘ　　　30　Ⓐ　Ⓑ　Ⓒ　Ⓓ

31　Ⓕ　Ⓖ　Ⓗ　Ⓘ　　　32　Ⓐ　Ⓑ　Ⓒ　Ⓓ　　　33　Ⓕ　Ⓖ　Ⓗ　Ⓘ

34　Ⓐ　Ⓑ　Ⓒ　Ⓓ　　　35　Ⓕ　Ⓖ　Ⓗ　Ⓘ　　　36　Ⓐ　Ⓑ　Ⓒ　Ⓓ

Fold and Tear Carefully Along Dotted Line.

37 Organisms all require food to provide the energy needed for the basic processes of life. What is the name for organisms that obtain their food directly from the Sun? How do these organisms make their food?

READ
INQUIRE
EXPLAIN

_____

_____

_____

_____

_____

38 Ⓕ Ⓖ Ⓗ Ⓘ   **39** Ⓐ Ⓑ Ⓒ Ⓓ   **40** Ⓕ Ⓖ Ⓗ Ⓘ

41 Ⓐ Ⓑ Ⓒ Ⓓ   **42** Ⓕ Ⓖ Ⓗ Ⓘ   **43** Ⓐ Ⓑ Ⓒ Ⓓ

44 Ⓕ Ⓖ Ⓗ Ⓘ   **45** Ⓐ Ⓑ Ⓒ Ⓓ   **46** Ⓕ Ⓖ Ⓗ Ⓘ

47 Ⓐ Ⓑ Ⓒ Ⓓ   **48** Ⓕ Ⓖ Ⓗ Ⓘ   **49** Ⓐ Ⓑ Ⓒ Ⓓ

Fold and Tear Carefully Along Dotted Line.

Go On ▶

This is the end of the Science Practice Tutorial—Answer Sheet.
Until time is called, go back and check your work or answer questions you
did not complete. When you have finished, close your workbook.

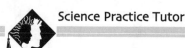

Blank Page

Science
Assessment One

Science Assessment One

Directions for Taking the Science Assessment One

On this section of the Florida Comprehensive Assessment Test (FCAT), you will answer 50 questions.

For multiple-choice questions, you will be asked to pick the best answer out of four possible choices and fill in the answer in the answer bubble. On gridded-response questions, you will also fill in your answer in answer bubbles, but you will fill in numbers and symbols corresponding to the solution you obtain for a question. Fill in the answer bubbles and gridded-response answer bubbles on the Answer Sheets on pages 191–197 to mark your selection.

For "Read, Inquire, Explain" questions (short- and extended-response items) you will put your answers on the Answer Sheets, but be sure to show your work on your Answer Sheet because you will be scored on your work as well as on your answer.

Read each question carefully and answer it to the best of your ability. If you do not know an answer, you may skip the question and come back to it later.

Figures and diagrams with given lengths and/or dimensions are not drawn to scale. Angle measures should be assumed to be accurate. Use the Science Reference Sheet on page 37 and the Periodic Table on page 38 to help you answer the questions.

When you finish, check your answers.

1 **READ INQUIRE EXPLAIN**   Go to your Science Assessment One Answer Sheet to answer Number 1.

2 The molecules in an object or a substance are always in motion. This kinetic energy can be measured and it varies from substance to substance. Which of the following would have the **highest** average kinetic energy?

    A. room temperature tap water
    B. an ice cube
    C. a cup of warm tomato soup
    D. a pot of boiling water

3 Water, a liquid, can exist in other forms. In the glass below, you can see liquid water, solid ice cubes, and water vapor that rises above the glass as a gas.

In which of these forms are the water molecules farthest apart from each other.

    F. in the ice cubes
    G. in the liquid water
    H. in the vapor
    I. The molecules are the same distance apart in all forms.

4 Which of the following is a physical change?

    A. digesting a meal
    B. boiling water
    C. burning newspaper
    D. baking bread

5 . Atoms that gain or lose electrons are called ions. Ions can have positive or negative charges of various strengths. Consider an ion with a weak negative charge. To which of the following would the ion with the **weak** negative charge be most attracted?

    F. It would be attracted to an ion with the same weak negative charge.
    G. It would be attracted to an ion with a stronger negative charge.
    H. It would be attracted to an ion with a weak positive charge.
    I. The charge of ions does not affect their attraction.

6 | READ INQUIRE EXPLAIN | Go to your Science Assessment One Answer Sheet to answer Number 6.

7 Light bulbs are designed to convert electric energy to light energy. Some light bulbs are more efficient than others are. When comparing two light bulbs, the more efficient bulb will produce less of what?

A. light
B. electricity
C. photons
D. heat

8 When an object that is at a high temperature comes in contact with an object of low temperature, thermal energy flows from the object of high temperature to the object of low temperature. This transfer can occur through a number of means. Which of the following energy flows is illustrated below, as heat from a flame flows to a metal bar that is in physical contact with it?

F. conduction
G. convection
H. radiation
I. expansion

9 Waves consist of many crests and troughs, but waves may be different in size and spacing. The waves on the left have higher crests than the waves on the right. The high crest also means the waves on the left have a higher

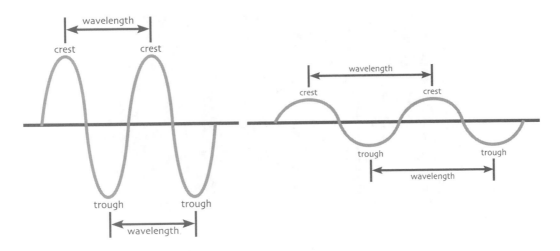

   A. wavelength.
   B. frequency.
   C. amplitude.
   D. peak.

10 One of the fundamental laws of physics says that the entropy of the universe must always increase. However, your body is constantly decreasing entropy within you (e.g., building of a protein, replicating DNA). How is this possible?

   F. The law about entropy only applies to chemical reactions.
   G. The definition of life is that which defies the entropy law.
   H. The entropy outside your body increases more than the entropy in your body decreases.
   I. Entropy is allowed to decrease for short periods of time as long as it eventually increases.

11 One of the many characteristics of an object in motion is acceleration. What information would you need to know in order to calculate an object's acceleration?

   A. the object's starting velocity and total time
   B. the object's total distance traveled and total time
   C. the object's starting and ending velocity and total time
   D. the object's starting and ending velocity and direction

12 In the solar system, the planets are millions of miles from the Sun, yet the Sun is still able to affect a planet's movement through space. For example, the planet Mercury moves in a constant orbit around the Sun as shown below.

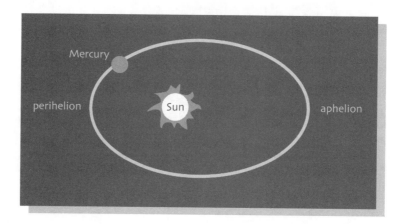

What force allows the Sun to have this effect on Mercury?

F. magnetism
G. electricity
H. momentum
I. gravity

13 Which of the following is **not** a machine?

A. screw
B. seesaw
C. can opener
D. candleholder

14  Go to your Science Assessment One Answer Sheet to answer Number 14.

15 The force of gravity between two objects is proportional to the objects'

F. size.
G. mass.
H. speed.
I. color.

Go On ▶

16 Most of Earth is covered in water, and life would not be possible without water. Water affects the planet in many ways. Which of the following was **not** formed by flowing water?

    A. the Grand Canyon
    B. the smooth sides of pebbles at a beach
    C. piles of dirt and silt at the mouth of a river
    D. the glacial ice caps

17 Local weather patterns are affected by the movement of large masses of air. When a mass of warm air moves into an area and pushes out a mass of cold air, a meteorologist will demonstrate it using the weather map shown below.

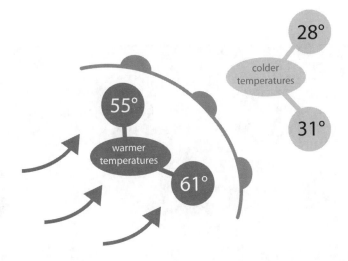

What is being shown arriving on the weather map?

    F. cold front
    G. warm front
    H. stationary front
    I. moveable front

18 If a forest suddenly loses all of its decomposers, which of the following would you expect to **decrease**?

    A. the amount nutrients in the soil
    B. the death rate of larger animals
    C. the ability of water to cycle through the system
    D. the amount of organic material on the soil's surface

19 In which of the following are the distances correctly listed from shortest to longest?

   F. the width of a blood cell, the space between carbon atoms in a diamond, the depth of the Pacific Ocean, the distance from Earth to the Moon
   G. the depth of the Pacific Ocean, the distance from Earth to the Moon, the width of a blood cell, the space between carbon atoms in a diamond
   H. the space between carbon atoms in a diamond, the width of a blood cell, the depth of the Pacific Ocean, the distance from Earth to the Moon
   I. the space between carbon atoms in a diamond, the width of a blood cell, the distance from Earth to the Moon, the depth of the Pacific Ocean

20 What unit is **most** commonly used to measure the distance between objects on the star map shown below?

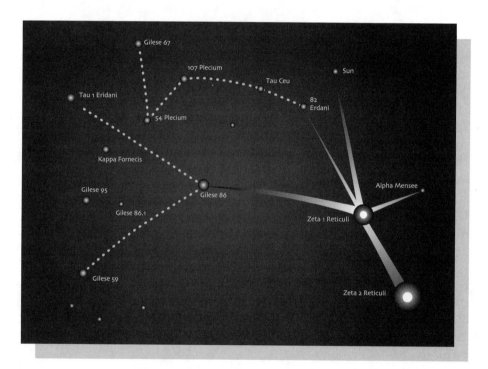

   A. miles
   B. light-years
   C. solar days
   D. kilometers

21 The amount of gas and dust that is collected during a star's formation affects the star's size as well as the temperature at the surface of the star, which affects the star's color. The larger the mass of the new star, the brighter and hotter it will be. Which of the following is **true** about the life of a star?

    F. A star with a larger mass exists longer than a star with a smaller mass.

    G. A star with a larger mass exists the same amount of time as a star with a smaller mass.

    H. A star with a smaller mass exists longer than a star with a larger mass.

    I. A star's initial mass does not affect how long the star will exist.

22 Our solar system has a Sun and nine planets. The third planet, Earth, is covered in water and supports life.

Which feature of our solar system would you be most likely to find in a solar system millions of light-years away?

    A. water

    B. life

    C. nine planets

    D. a sun

23 Which body system, shown below, allows your body to transport nutrients to all of your cells?

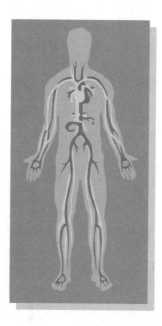

   F. respiratory system
   G. digestive system
   H. circulatory system
   I. endocrine system

24 Living things come in many shapes and sizes. Why is the person shown below so much larger than the ant?

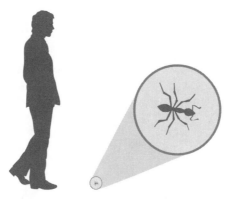

   A. because the human's cells are larger than the ant's
   B. because the ant's cells are more tightly packed than the human's
   C. because the human's cells are stretched out
   D. because the ant has fewer cells than the human

25 Which of the following is **not** a function of mitosis?

    F. create diversity within the organism
    G. increase the overall size of an organism
    H. aid in injury repair
    I. replace old cells

26 The cells that line the inside of the small intestine have finger-like projections called microvilli. How do these structures affect the function of the organ?

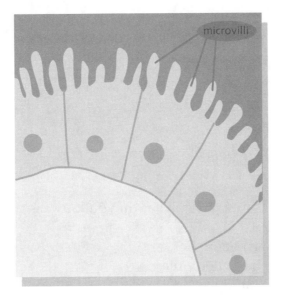

    A. They allow the organ to absorb more nutrients from food.
    B. They cause the food to travel more slowly through the organ.
    C. They prevent the organ from absorbing unhealthy food contents.
    D. They allow the organ to detect the content of the food within it.

27 Cells in the leaf and stem of a plant cell can convert energy from light into chemical energy during photosynthesis. However, there are some plant cells (a root cell for example) that, if exposed to light, will not be able to undergo photosynthesis. Why are some plant cells unable to perform photosynthesis?

    F. There are plant cells that are killed by light exposure.
    G. Not all cells need energy, so not all cells use photosynthesis.
    H. Since all cells are connected, photosynthesis only occurs in certain cells.
    I. Not all cells have the structure that is required for the conversion of light to energy.

Go On ▶

28 A red flower is mated with a white flower and produces offspring that are all pink flowers. This is an example of what type of dominance?

A. incomplete dominance
B. negative dominance
C. reverse dominance
D. complete dominance

29 If two species are in the same order, what do you know is **true**?

F. They share specific characteristics.
G. They share the same basic body plan.
H. They are in the same family.
I. They can interbreed.

30 Nitrogen is one of the most common elements on the planet. What is meant by the phrase "nitrogen fixation"?

A. Nitrogen is converted from a gas form to a form that organisms can use.
B. Bonds between nitrogen atoms are repaired to increase stability.
C. Nitrogen is released into the atmosphere by plants.
D. Nitrogen is consumed by aquatic organisms.

31 Which of the following sources of energy came from living organisms?

    F. oil
    G. nuclear power
    H. geothermal energy
    I. solar energy

32 Plants and animals live in very complicated environments that are composed of both living and non-living parts, many of which affect each other in numerous ways. Of the following non-living factors in an environment, which one is **not** affected by the others?

    A. humidity
    B. air temperature
    C. rainfall
    D. soil depth

33 When a population of wolves gets too large, which of the following will cause the population size to **decrease**?

    F. disease
    G. predation
    H. limiting abiotic and biotic resources
    I. increasing habitat

34 Many state and national parks contain areas that are "undisturbed environments." What is meant by "undisturbed"?

    A. The area has not been affected by humans.
    B. The area contains many species not found elsewhere.
    C. The area only contains species that are not useful to humans.
    D. The area only contains species that are useful to humans.

35 Many decades ago, scientists observed long, straight features on the surface of Mars. Many scientists felt that these features must be made by intelligent beings, since they were so large and straight. They called them "canals" and made a case that intelligent life may have existed on Mars. Today scientists know that these are not canals built by life forms.

What caused this theory to be discarded?

    F. New technology has allowed scientists to discover more information about the features.
    G. Scientists have developed new theories that are more important than these observations.
    H. Scientists have ignored these observations in order to develop different theories.
    I. Scientists realized that they could not trust new technologies.

36 A scientist is conducting an experiment to determine how much a local species of butterfly will be affected by the pesticide put on vegetable gardens to keep harmful beetles away. Which of the following would be **most** useful in helping the scientist develop a hypothesis?

   A. the effects of the pesticide on the harmful beetles
   B. the way in which the beetles get into the gardens
   C. the likelihood of the butterflies to feed in the gardens
   D. the effects of the pesticides on the vegetables in the gardens

37 The subjects studied in biology are very different from those studied in geology. Why would the methods used by a geologist seem very familiar to a biologist?

   F. Both subjects require a basic knowledge of the other.
   G. Both subjects use methods based on the same scientific philosophies.
   H. Scientists often use both subjects to reach a single conclusion.
   I. Both subjects use similar tools to collect data and reach conclusions.

38   Go to your Science Assessment One Answer Sheet to answer Number 38.

39 In an experiment, which of the following is **not** directly controlled by the person conducting the experiment?

A. independent variable
B. dependent variable
C. hypothesis
D. constant conditions

40 It has been known for many years that specific types of radiation are very dangerous to people. However, there has not been as much research on these effects as there has been in many other areas of medical research. Why would scientists **not** study this?

F. It is difficult to study these effects without harming people.
G. The dangerous types of radiation are all very rare.
H. Scientists do not consider the issue worthwhile.
I. Radiation is a difficult and confusing subject.

41 Which of the following measurements is being taken?

    A. area
    B. mass
    C. volume
    D. weight

42 What is Kyle measuring with the thermometer?

    F. the mass of the particles that make up the air
    G. the amount of light energy bouncing off air particles
    H. the volume of space between the particles that make up air
    I. the average energy of motion in the air particles

43 Which part of the atom is indicated by the arrow below?

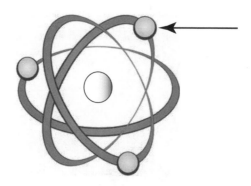

A. electron
B. neutron
C. nucleus
D. proton

44 Which of the following activities describes a chemical change?

F. liquid water freezes to solid ice
G. 5 mL of orange juice is added to 3 mL of orange juice
H. a bowl of sand is poured into a square jar
I. a piece of wood is burned in a fire

Go On

45 Which property of a wave is being measured below?

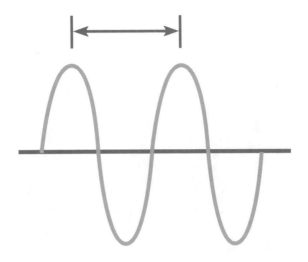

A. amplitude
B. phase shift
C. frequency
D. wavelength

46 Go to your Science Assessment One Answer Sheet to answer Number 46.

47 Which of the following properties are shared by the sand in the beaker and the water in the graduated cylinder?

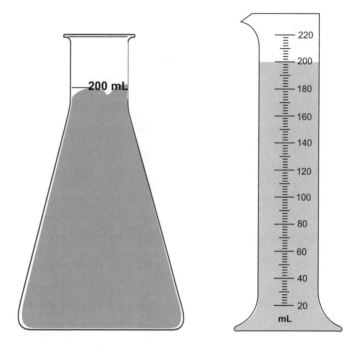

F. The sand and water both have the same mass.

G. The sand and water both have the same physical state.

H. The sand and water both have the same volume.

I. The sand and water both have the same weight.

48 Cars are often described by their fuel efficiency. The most efficient cars use more of the energy released from burning gasoline to cause motion. What happens to the energy in gasoline that is **not** used to make the car move?

    A. It is destroyed.
    B. It returns to gasoline.
    C. It becomes exhaust.
    D. It is transformed into heat.

49 Which of the following is **not** a form of energy that we receive from the Sun?

    F. visible light
    G. chemical
    H. infrared
    I. microwave

50 Where does the energy from the fossil fuels such as coal and oil that we use come from?

    A. metals
    B. minerals
    C. organisms
    D. sand

This is the end of the Science Assessment One.
Until time is called, go back and check your work or answer
questions you did not complete. When you have finished, close
your workbook.

Answer Sheet

Name_____

Science Assessment One Answer Sheet

Answer all the questions that appear in Science Assessment One on this Answer Sheet. Answer multiple-choice questions by filling in the bubble for the answer you select. Answer gridded-response questions by filling in the correct bubbles. Write your answers to "Read, Inquire, Explain" questions on the lines provided.

To remove your Answer Sheet, carefully tear along the dotted line.

Fold and Tear Carefully Along Dotted Line.

1 Christine looked up the definition of density in her science book. The book defined density as a physical property of matter that can be found by dividing the mass of a material by its volume. She decided to do an experiment to see if a substance could have different densities depending on its state. First, she measured a liter of water and placed it in a pan. Then she measured a liter of water, poured it into ice cube trays, and froze it in the freezer. Next she emptied the ice cubes into the liter of water and observed the ice floating. The water left as liquid and the water frozen as ice had the same mass. Explain which has the greater density, ice or water, and why the density of the water apparently changed when it was frozen.

READ
INQUIRE
EXPLAIN

_____

_____

_____

_____

_____

2 Ⓐ Ⓑ Ⓒ Ⓓ   **3** Ⓕ Ⓖ Ⓗ Ⓘ   **4** Ⓐ Ⓑ Ⓒ Ⓓ

5 Ⓕ Ⓖ Ⓗ Ⓘ

Fold and Tear Carefully Along Dotted Line.

6 Many people like wind energy production because it does not have the by-products of some of the other forms of energy production. However, it requires space for large windmills, and some people feel it is not as efficient as some other forms of energy production.

READ
INQUIRE
EXPLAIN

Identify two categories of energy involved in wind energy production and briefly explain the process.

_____

_____

_____

_____

_____

Go On

7 Ⓐ Ⓑ Ⓒ Ⓓ　　　　**8** Ⓕ Ⓖ Ⓗ Ⓘ　　　　**9** Ⓐ Ⓑ Ⓒ Ⓓ

10 Ⓕ Ⓖ Ⓗ Ⓘ　　　　**11** Ⓐ Ⓑ Ⓒ Ⓓ　　　　**12** Ⓕ Ⓖ Ⓗ Ⓘ

13 Ⓐ Ⓑ Ⓒ Ⓓ

14 Imagine that you are holding a heavy book out in front of you. The book is motionless. Why is the book **not** moving?

READ
INQUIRE
EXPLAIN

_____

_____

_____

_____

_____

15 Ⓕ Ⓖ Ⓗ Ⓘ　　　　**16** Ⓐ Ⓑ Ⓒ Ⓓ　　　　**17** Ⓕ Ⓖ Ⓗ Ⓘ

18 Ⓐ Ⓑ Ⓒ Ⓓ　　　　**19** Ⓕ Ⓖ Ⓗ Ⓘ　　　　**20** Ⓐ Ⓑ Ⓒ Ⓓ

21 Ⓕ Ⓖ Ⓗ Ⓘ　　　　**22** Ⓐ Ⓑ Ⓒ Ⓓ　　　　**23** Ⓕ Ⓖ Ⓗ Ⓘ

Fold and Tear Carefully Along Dotted Line.

Go On ▶

24 Ⓐ Ⓑ Ⓒ Ⓓ   **25** Ⓕ Ⓖ Ⓗ Ⓘ   **26** Ⓐ Ⓑ Ⓒ Ⓓ

27 Ⓕ Ⓖ Ⓗ Ⓘ   **28** Ⓐ Ⓑ Ⓒ Ⓓ   **29** Ⓕ Ⓖ Ⓗ Ⓘ

30 Ⓐ Ⓑ Ⓒ Ⓓ   **31** Ⓕ Ⓖ Ⓗ Ⓘ   **32** Ⓐ Ⓑ Ⓒ Ⓓ

33 Ⓕ Ⓖ Ⓗ Ⓘ   **34** Ⓐ Ⓑ Ⓒ Ⓓ   **35** Ⓕ Ⓖ Ⓗ Ⓘ

36 Ⓐ Ⓑ Ⓒ Ⓓ   **37** Ⓕ Ⓖ Ⓗ Ⓘ

38 How does scientific theory affect established scientific knowledge and old observations?

READ
INQUIRE
EXPLAIN

_____

_____

_____

_____

_____

_____

_____

_____

_____

Fold and Tear Carefully Along Dotted Line.

Go On ▶

39 Ⓐ Ⓑ Ⓒ Ⓓ   **40** Ⓕ Ⓖ Ⓗ Ⓘ   **41** Ⓐ Ⓑ Ⓒ Ⓓ

42 Ⓕ Ⓖ Ⓗ Ⓘ   **43** Ⓐ Ⓑ Ⓒ Ⓓ   **44** Ⓕ Ⓖ Ⓗ Ⓘ

45 Ⓐ Ⓑ Ⓒ Ⓓ

Fold and Tear Carefully Along Dotted Line.

Go On ▶

46 Describe the three different transfers of energy that occur in the scenario shown below.

READ
INQUIRE
EXPLAIN

_____

_____

_____

_____

_____

47 F   G   H   I   **48** A   B   C   D   **49** F   G   H   I

50 A   B   C   D

Go On

This is the end of the Science Assessment One—Answer Sheet.
Until time is called, go back and check your work or answer questions you did not complete. When you have finished, close your workbook.

Science Assessment One—Skills Chart

Question	Standard	Answer	Keywords
1	SC.A.1.3.1	see analysis	Ways in which substances differ
2	SC.A.1.3.3	D	Temperature measures average energy of motion of particles that make up the substance
3	SC.A.1.3.4	H	Atoms and solids are close together and do not move around easily
4	SC.A.1.3.5	B	Physical change in a substance
5	SC.A.2.3.2	H	Properties of the atom
6	SC.B.1.3.1	see analysis	Forms of energy
7	SC.B.1.3.4	D	Energy conversions are never 100% efficient
8	SC.B.1.3.5	F	Processes of thermal energy
9	SC.B.1.3.6	C	Properties of waves
10	SC.B.2.3.1	H	Energy transfer
11	SC.C.1.3.1	C	Motion of an object can be described by its position, direction of motion, and speed
12	SC.C.2.3.1	I	Many forces act at a distance
13	SC.C.2.3.4	D	Simple machines can be used to change direction or size of a force
14	SC.C.2.3.6	see analysis	Net force can act on an object
15	SC.C.2.3.7	G	Gravity
16	SC.D.1.3.1	D	Mechanical and chemical activities shape and reshape Earth's surface
17	SC.D.1.3.3	G	Conditions exist in one system influence the conditions that exist in other systems
18	SC.D.1.3.4	A	Ways in which plants and animals reshape the landscape
19	SC.D.1.3.5	H	Concepts of time and size relating to the interaction of Earth's processes
20	SC.E.1.3.1	B	Vast size of our Solar System
21	SC.E.1.3.4	H	Stars appear to be made of similar elements
22	SC.E.2.3.1	D	Other galaxies appear similar in element, forces, and energy found in our Solar System
23	SC.F.1.3.1	H	Living things are composed of systems that function in reproduction, growth, maintenance, and regulation
24	SC.F.1.3.2	D	Organisms that a single celled and Multicellular
25	SC.F.1.3.3	F	Multicellular organisms

Science Assessment One—Skills Chart

Question	Standard	Answer	Keywords
26	SC.F.1.3.5	A	Life functions of organisms are related to what occurs with the cell
27	SC.F.1.3.6	I	Functions of cells
28	SC.F.2.3.2	A	Variation in species due to genetic information passed from parent to offspring
29	SC.G.1.3.3	F	Classification of living things
30	SC.G.1.3.4	A	Interactions resulting in the flow of energy and the cycling of matter throughout a system
31	SC.G.2.3.1	F	Renewable and nonrenewable resources
32	SC.G.2.3.2	D	Biotic and abiotic factors
33	SC.G.2.3.3	H	Change in resource may alter size of population
34	SC.G.2.3.4	A	Humans are part of an ecosystem and their activities may alter the equilibrium in ecosystems
35	SC.H.1.3.1	F	Scientific knowledge is subject to modification
36	SC.H.1.3.2	C	Study of events that led scientists to discoveries can provide information about the process and effects
37	SC.H.1.3.1	G	New information challenges prevailing theories
38	SC.H.1.3.4	see analysis	Accurate record keeping, openness, and replication are essential to credibility
39	SC.H.1.3.5	B	Change in one or more variables may alter outcome of an investigation
40	SC.H.3.3.1	F	Science ethics
41	SC.A.1.3.2	B	Weight and mass
42	SC.A.1.3.3	I	Temperature measures the average energy of motion of the particles that make up a substance
43	SC.A.2.3.2	A	Radiation, heat, and light are forms of energy
44	SC.A.1.3.5	I	Processes of thermal energy
45	SC.B.1.3.6	A	Properties of waves
46	SC.B.1.3.3	see analysis	Forms of energy from the sun
47	SC.A.1.3.6	H	Equal volumes of different substances may have different masses
48	SC.B.1.3.4	D	Energy conversions are never 100% efficient
49	SC.B.1.3.3	G	Forms of energy from the Sun
50	SC.B.2.3.2	C	Energy forms used today derived from burning stored energy collected millions of years ago

           © Englefield & Associates, Inc.

Science Assessment One—Answer Key

1 Christine looked up the definition of density in her science book. The book defined density as a physical property of matter that can be found by dividing the mass of a material by its volume. She decided to do an experiment to see if a substance could have different densities depending on its state. First, she measured a liter of water and placed it in a pan. Then she measured a liter of water, poured it into ice cube trays, and froze it in the freezer. Next she emptied the ice cubes into the liter of water and observed the ice floating. The water left as liquid and the water frozen as ice had the same mass. Explain which has the greater density, ice or water, and why the density of the water apparently changed when it was frozen.
Analysis: Water has a greater density than ice. The experiment proves this. The reason ice floats is because it is less dense than water. Both volumes of water started out with the same volume and mass, so they had the same density. However, water expands as it freezes, so the denominator in the definition of density,

$$density = \frac{mass}{volume}$$

gets larger which makes the ice less dense.

2 The molecules in an object or a substance are always in motion. This kinetic energy can be measured and it varies from substance to substance. Which of the following would have the **highest** average kinetic energy?
Analysis: *Choice D is correct.* Temperature is a measure of average kinetic energy, so the substance with the highest temperature will have the highest average kinetic energy. Choices A, B, and C are all incorrect because they all have a lower temperature than boiling water.

3 Water, a liquid, can exist in other forms. In the glass below, you can see liquid water, solid ice cubes, and water vapor that rises above the glass as a gas.

In which of these forms are the water molecules **farthest** apart from each other.
Analysis: *Choice H is correct.* Molecules in solids are closely packed. They are usually farther apart in liquids and even farther apart in gases. Choices F and G are incorrect. Choice I is incorrect because a state is defined by the movement and spacing of molecules.

4 Which of the following is a physical change?
Analysis: *Choice B is correct.* A physical change is one in which a physical quality of a substance is changed but the chemical qualities are unchanged. Boiling water only changes the form from a liquid to a gas. Choice A is incorrect because the digestive system changes the apple into a substance that the body can use. Choice C is incorrect because burning paper chemically changes the paper into ashes. Choice D is incorrect because the baking of bread is a chemical change.

5 Atoms that gain or lose electrons are called ions. Ions can have positive or negative charges of various strengths. Consider an ion with a weak negative charge. To which of the following would the ion with the **weak** negative charge be most attracted?
Analysis: *Choice H is correct.* In the case of ions, opposite charges attract. Choices F and G are incorrect because the negatively charged ions would repel each other. Choice I is incorrect because the attraction between ions is determined almost entirely by charge.

6 Many people like wind energy production because it does not have the by-products of some of the other forms of energy production. However, it requires space for large windmills, and some people feel it is not as efficient as some other forms of energy production.

Identify two categories of energy involved in wind energy production and briefly explain the process.
Analysis: *Short-response answers may vary.* Windmills take the kinetic energy of the wind and convert it to a useable electric form. Therefore, energy is converted from kinetic energy to electrical energy.

Science Assessment One—Answer Key

7 Light bulbs are designed to convert electric energy to light energy. Some light bulbs are more efficient than others are. When comparing two light bulbs, the more efficient bulb will produce less of what?

Analysis: *Choice D is correct.* In the transfer that converts electric energy to light energy, some energy is lost as heat. The most inefficient bulb will lose the most energy as heat. Choices A and C are incorrect because the most efficient bulb will produce the most light (and photons), not the least. Choice B is incorrect because bulbs use electricity, they do not produce it.

8 When an object that is at a high temperature comes in contact with an object of low temperature, thermal energy flows from the object of high temperature to the object of low temperature. This transfer can occur through a number of means. Which of the following energy flows is illustrated below, as heat from a flame flows to a metal bar that is in physical contact with it?

Analysis: *Choice F is correct.* The transfer of thermal energy by physical contact is conduction. Choice G is incorrect because convection is the transfer of thermal energy by the movement of a liquid or gas. Choice H is incorrect because radiation is the transfer of thermal energy through space. Choice I is

incorrect because expansion is not a term used in the field of thermal energy transfer.

9 Waves consist of many crests and trough, but waves may be different in size and spacing. The waves on the left have higher crests than the waves on the right. The higher crest also means the waves on the left have a higher

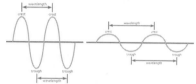

Analysis: *Choice C is correct.* Amplitude is a measure of the height of a wave. Choice A is incorrect because wavelength is a measure of the width of a wave. Choice B is incorrect because frequency is the rate at which crests occur. Choice D is incorrect because peak refers to the point at which the wave is highest, but does not reflect anything about what that height is.

10 One of the fundamental laws of physics says that the entropy of the universe must always increase. However, your body is constantly decreasing entropy within you (e.g., building of a protein, replicating DNA). How is this possible?
Analysis: *Choice H is correct.* The entropy of the entire universe must increase, so if entropy decreases locally (inside your body) it must increase outside the local system (outside your body). Choices F and G are incorrect because the entropy law (the second law of thermodynamics) applies to all reactions—chemical, organic, or otherwise. Choice I is incorrect because the entropy of the universe must be increasing at all times.

11 One of the many characteristics of an object in motion is acceleration. What information would you need to know in order to calculate an object's acceleration?
Analysis: *Choice C is correct.* Acceleration can be calculated by dividing the change in velocity by the total time. Choice A is incorrect because an ending velocity is needed. Choice B is incorrect because total distance and total time can show average velocity, but not acceleration. Choice D is incorrect because a total distance is required for the calculation of acceleration.

12 In the solar system, the planets are millions of miles away from the Sun, yet the Sun is sill able to affect a planet's movement through space. For example, the planet Mercury moves in a constant orbit around the Sun as shown below.

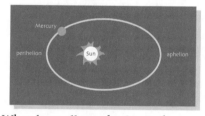

What force allows the Sun to have this effect on Mercury?
Analysis: *Choice I is correct.* The planets' orbits are determined by the Sun's gravitational field. Choices F and G are incorrect because they do not affect orbits. Choice H is incorrect because, although momentum may help keep a planet moving, it does not relate to the effects of the Sun.

Science Assessment One—Answer Key

13 Which of the following is **not** a machine?
Analysis: *Choice D is correct.* The candleholder is the only item that does not reduce the work required for a task. Choice A is incorrect because a screw is an inclined plane wound around an axis. Choice B is incorrect because a seesaw is a lever. Choice C is incorrect because a can opener is a complex machine that reduces the work required to open a can.

14 Imagine that you are holding a heavy book out in front of you. The book is motionless. Why is the book **not** moving?
Analysis: *Short-response answers may vary.* The force of gravity acting downward on the book is balanced by the upward force of the hand holding the book. The forces acting upon the book are balanced and that is why the book is not moving.

15 The force of gravity between two objects is proportional to the objects'
Analysis: *Choice G is correct.* The force of gravity between two objects is directly related to the objects' combined mass. Choices F, H, and I are incorrect because these are not factors that affect the force of gravity between two objects.

16 Most of Earth is covered in water, and life would not be possible without water. Water affects the planet in many ways. Which of the following was **not** formed by flowing water?
Analysis: *Choice D is correct.* The glacial ice caps are made of water, but were not formed by flowing water. Choice A is incorrect because the Grand Canyon was formed by the flowing Colorado River. Choice B is incorrect because the beach pebbles were smoothed by the ocean waves. Choice C is incorrect because the dirt and silt are deposited by the flowing river.

17 Local weather patterns are affected by the movement of large masses of air. When a mass of warm air moves into an area and pushes out a mass of cold air, a meteorologist will demonstrate it using the weather map shown below.

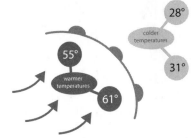

What is being shown arriving on the weather map?
Analysis: *Choice G is correct.* A warm front is when warm air replaces cold air. Choice F is incorrect because a cold front is when cold air replaces warm air. Choice H is incorrect because a stationary front is when a large mass of air is relatively still. Choice I is incorrect because "moveable front" is not a term used in meteorology.

18 If a forest suddenly loses all of its decomposers, which of the following would you expect to **decrease**?
Analysis: *Choice A is correct.* Decomposers help to cycle nutrients from dead organisms back into the soil. Choice B is incorrect because a lack of nutrients in the soil may increase the death rate, but it would not decrease it. Choice C is incorrect because decomposers are not a part of the water cycle. Choice D is incorrect because dead organic material would build up (i.e., increase) on the soil's surface without decomposers there to break it down.

19 In which of the following are the distances correctly listed from shortest to longest?
Analysis: *Choice H is correct.* The distance between atoms is measured in angstroms. The width of a cell is measured in nanometers. The depth of the Pacific Ocean is measured in kilometers. The distance from the Earth to the moon is measured in thousands of kilometers.

20 What unit is **most** commonly used to measure the distance between objects on the star map shown below?

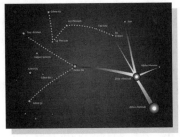

Analysis: *Choice B is correct.* A light-year is the standard unit of measure in the galaxy. Choices A and D are too small to be useful. Choice C is not a measure of distance.

21 The amount of gas and dust that is collected during a star's formation affects the star's size as well as the temperature at the surface of the star, which affects the star's color. The larger the mass of the new star, the brighter and hotter it will be. Which of the following is **true** about the life of a star?
Analysis: *Choice H is correct.* Stars with large initial masses start out as very bright and very hot stars; the number of reactions taking place in the cores of these massive stars is greater than that of smaller stars. Because massive stars need more fuel for their greater number of reactions, they run out of fuel (the main fuel of stars is hydrogen) more quickly than stars with less mass.

Copying is Prohibited

Science Assessment One—Answer Key

22 Our solar system has a Sun and nine planets. The third planet, Earth, is covered in water and supports life.

Which feature of our solar system would you be most likely to find in a solar system millions of light-years away?

Analysis: *Choice D is correct.* All solar systems involve planets orbiting a sun, which is a star. Choice A is incorrect because water is not on all planets and, therefore, may not be on the planets in another system. Choice B is incorrect because we have yet to find any evidence of life outside of Earth. Choice C is incorrect because solar systems may have any number of planets, not just nine.

23 Which body system, shown below, allows your body to transport nutrients to all of your cells?

Analysis: *Choice H is correct.* The circulatory system is the system of the heart and blood. Choice A is incorrect because the respiratory system deals with bringing in oxygen and getting rid of carbon dioxide. Choice G is incorrect because the digestive system only involves the breakdown and absorption of nutrients, not their transport. Choice I is incorrect because the endocrine system deals with the production and release of hormones in the body.

24 Living things come in many shapes and sizes. Why is the person shown below so much larger than the ant?

Analysis: *Choice D is correct.* The size of an organism is directly related to the number of cells within the organism. Choice A is incorrect. Although cells do vary in size, this variation occurs within an individual organism and is not nearly dramatic enough to account for differences in size of the organisms in the question—an ant and a person. Choice B is incorrect because the spacing between cells varies only very slightly. Choice C is incorrect because cells rarely stretch and stretching would have no effect on size.

25 Which of the following is **not** a function of mitosis?

Analysis: *Choice F is correct.* Mitosis creates two identical cells (both are identical to each other as well as to the original), so there is no diversity created. Choice G is incorrect since mitosis increases the number of cells present. Choice H is incorrect since mitosis occurs around injuries. Choice I is incorrect because one of the most common functions of mitosis is to maintain the number of cells in the organism by replacing old and dying cells.

26 The cells that line the inside of the small intestine have finger-like projections called microvilli. How do these structures affect the function of the organ?

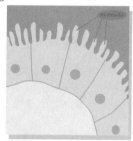

Analysis: *Choice A is correct.* The microvilli increase the cells' surface areas and, therefore, the ability to absorb material. Choice B is incorrect because the microvilli only protrude slightly into the interior of the organ and would not affect the speed of the food's travel. Choice C is incorrect because the microvilli do not change the specificity of the absorption. Choice D is incorrect because the microvilli do not have any ability to detect anything from the interior of the organ.

27 Cells in the leaf and stem of a plant cell can convert energy from light into chemical energy during photosynthesis. However, there are some plant cells (a root cell for example) that, if exposed to light, will not be able to undergo photosynthesis. Why are some plant cells unable to perform photosynthesis?

Analysis: *Choice I is correct.* Some cells lack chloroplasts, which are the structures that perform photosynthesis. Choice F is incorrect; this does not explain why some cells can't perform photosynthesis. Choice G is incorrect because all cells require energy to function. Choice H is incorrect because, although cells are connected, the connection is not a reason why some cells are unable to perform a certain function.

Science Assessment One—Answer Key

28 A red flower is mated with a white flower and produces offspring that are all pink flowers. This is an example of what type of dominance?

Analysis: *Choice A is correct.* Incomplete dominance is when both the characteristics of the parents are expressed at the same time. Choices B and C are not terms used in heredity. Choice D is incorrect because complete dominance would lead to the creation of only red flowers.

29 If two species are in the same order, what do you know is **true**?
Analysis: *Choice F is correct.* All groupings, including orders, are defined by specific characteristics. Choice G is incorrect because the basic body plan is not necessarily one of the order's defining characteristics. Choice H is incorrect because family is a group within an order, so species in different families can be in the same order. Choice I is incorrect because different species cannot usually interbreed.

30 Nitrogen is one of the most common elements on the planet. What is meant by the phrase "nitrogen fixation"?
Analysis: *Choice A is correct.* "Nitrogen fixation" is a process in which decomposers convert nitrogen from an unusable form into a useable form. "Nitrogen fixation" is a specific process that does not include those described in choices B, C, and D.

31 Which of the following sources of energy came from living organisms?
Analysis: *Choice F is correct.* Fossil fuels were created by living organisms millions of years ago. Choice G is incorrect because nuclear power requires a chemical and physical reaction, not a biological one. Choice H is incorrect because geothermal energy is based only on the geological features of Earth. Choice I is incorrect because solar energy only requires sunlight.

32 Plants and animals live in very complicated environments that are composed of both living and non-living parts, many of which affect each other in numerous ways. Of the following non-living factors in an environment, which one is **not** affected by the others?
Analysis: *Choice D is correct.* Choice D is the only one not affected by the other factors listed. Choice A is incorrect because humidity is directly affected by both rainfall and temperature. Choice B is incorrect because air temperature is directly affected by both humidity and rainfall. Choice C is incorrect because rainfall is affected directly by humidity and indirectly by air temperature.

33 When a population of wolves gets too large, which of the following will cause the population size to **decrease**?
Analysis: *Choice H is correct.* When a population gets larger than its carrying capacity, limiting resources force the population back to the carrying capacity. Choice F is incorrect because disease is not strictly dependent on a large population size. Choice G is incorrect because wolves are not the victims of much predation. Choice I is incorrect because increasing habitat would be a way to increase population size, not decrease it.

34 Many state and national parks contain areas that are "undisturbed environments." What is meant by "undisturbed"?
Analysis: *Choice A is correct.* An "undisturbed" area is one that is as it was before humans affected the area. Choices B, C, and D are all incorrect because the term "undisturbed" says nothing about the species found in the area.

35 Many decades ago, scientists observed long, straight features on the surface of Mars. Many scientists felt that these features must be made by intelligent beings, since they were so large and straight. They called them "canals" and made a case that intelligent life may have existed on Mars. Today scientists know that these are not canals built by life forms.

What caused this theory to be discarded?
Analysis: *Choice F is correct.* Telescope technology and the development of unmanned probes has allowed scientists to discover more information about Mars. This information has allowed them to rule out the construction of these features by life forms. Choice G is incorrect because data was needed in order to back up new theories. Choice H is incorrect because scientists must use all observations and evidence to evaluate theories. Choice I is incorrect because the development of new technology often helps scientists gather more information.

Science Assessment One—Answer Key

36 A scientist is conducting an experiment to determine how much a local species of butterfly will be affected by the pesticide put on vegetable gardens to keep harmful beetles away. Which of the following would be **most** useful in helping the scientist develop a hypothesis?
Analysis: *Choice C is correct.* Choice C is the only one of these factors that has anything to do with the pesticide's effect on butterflies. Choice A is incorrect because the effect on the beetles is distinct from the possible effect on butterflies. Choice B is incorrect because the movement of the beetles is different from that of the butterflies. Choice D is incorrect because the effects on the vegetables may have no bearing on the possible effects on the butterflies.

37 The subjects studied in biology are very different from those studied in geology. Why would the methods used by a geologist seem very familiar to a biologist?
Analysis: *Choice G is correct.* All sciences use the same basic philosophies and methods. Choice F is incorrect because most research in either subject requires little to no knowledge of the other. Choice H is incorrect because there are only a few topics that use both subjects. Choice I is incorrect because the subjects use very different tools to collect data.

38 How does a new scientific theory affect established scientific knowledge and old observations?
Analysis: *Extended-response answers may vary.* New information adds to the knowledge that scientists have about a subject. If the new information reinforces or adds to a scientific theory, the theory is strengthened and expanded. It can often lead to new, improved investigations that add more information and understanding. If the new information contradicts the established information then it can cause scientists to reexamine the theory. It may disprove the theory or it may cause scientists to revise the theory or change direction in how they think about it.

39 In an experiment, which of the following is **not** directly controlled by the person conducting the experiment?
Analysis: *Choice B is correct.* The dependent variable is that which reacts to the independent variable. Choice A is incorrect because the independent variable is manipulated by the experimenter. Choice C is incorrect because the hypothesis is created by the individual conducting the experiment. Choice D is incorrect because the constant conditions are controlled and set by the experimenter.

40 It has been known for many years that specific types of radiation are very dangerous to people. However, there has not been as much research on these effects as there has been in many other areas of medical research. Why would scientists **not** study this?
Analysis: *Choice F is correct.* It is difficult to study the negative effects of anything on humans since scientists have an ethical obligation to not place anyone in harm. Choice G is incorrect because many dangerous types of radiation (e.g., UV, X-rays) are quite common. Choice H is incorrect because radiation sickness is a very serious medical issue. Choice I is incorrect because radiation sickness is not any more difficult a subject than many other medical subjects.

41 Which of the following measurements is being taken?

Analysis: *Choice B is correct.* A balance scale measures the mass of an object. Area is calculated by measuring the size of all outside areas of an object. Volume is measured with a graduated cylinder or similar container. Weight is measured using a scale that is calibrated to gravity.

Science Assessment One—Answer Key

42 What is Kyle measuring with the thermometer?

Analysis: *Choice I is correct.* (The average energy of motion in the air particles.) A thermometer measures temperature. The temperature of the air is a measurement of the energy of motion in the air particles. As the motion of air particles increases, the temperature increases. As the motion of air particles decreases, the temperature decreases. Temperature is not a measurement of air mass, light energy, or air volume.

43 Which part of the atom is indicated by the arrow below?

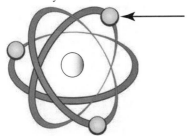

Analysis: *Choice A is correct.* Atoms are composed of electrons, neutrons, and protons. The electrons are negatively charged and orbit outside the nucleus. The protons are positively charged and are located within the nucleus. The neutrons are neutrally charged and located within the nucleus.

44 Which of the following activities describes a chemical change?
Analysis: *Choice I is correct.* A chemical change affects the composition of a substance. When a substance undergoes chemical change, it results in a new substance with different characteristics. Wood that is burned combines with oxygen to create carbon dioxide gas, along with some other gasses. Physical changes such as changing from a liquid to gas, a change in volume of the same substance, or change in shape do not create new substances with different characteristics.

45 Which property of a wave is being measured below?

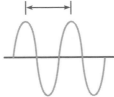

Analysis: *Choice D is correct.* A wavelength is measured from one point on a wave to the same point on the next wave. Choice A is incorrect. The amplitude of a wave is the measurement of its height. Choice C is incorrect. The frequency of the wave is a measurement of how many wavelengths occur during a time interval. Choice B is incorrect. A phase shift is a movement of a wave to the left or right.

46 Describe the transfer of energy that occurs in the scenario shown below.

Analysis: *Short-response questions may vary.* The correct answer is that light (or solar) energy from the sun is transferred to electrical energy that is carried through wires to a radio, where it is transferred to sound energy.

47 Which of the following properties are shared by the sand in the beaker and the water in the graduated cylinder?

Analysis: *Choice H is correct.* The sand and water both measure 200 mL in the beaker and graduated cylinder. This is a measurement of volume. Two different substances that have the same volumes most likely have different masses and weights. The two substances have different states, since one is solid and one is liquid.

Science Assessment One—Answer Key

48 Cars are often described by their fuel efficiency. The most efficient cars use more of the energy released from burning gasoline to cause motion. What happens to the energy in gasoline that is **not** used to make the car move?

Analysis: *Choice D is correct.* Energy cannot be destroyed or created. It can only be transformed. Some of the energy created by burning gasoline in a car's engine is converted to mechanical energy to move the car. Most of the energy, however, is lost as heat energy that is wasted. Energy is not changed back into gasoline, and exhaust is a waste product of all of the gasoline energy used.

49 Which of the following is **not** a form of energy that we receive from the Sun?

Analysis: *Choice G is correct.* The Sun supplies Earth with light energy and heat energy. The light energy is in the form of infrared, visible light, and microwave light waves. The Sun does not supply chemical energy, although solar energy can be converted into chemical energy by plants through photosynthesis.

50 Where does the energy from the fossil fuels such as coal and oil that we use come from?

Analysis: *Choice C is correct.* Coal and oil are created from decomposed organisms that have been compressed over millions of years. Coal and oil do not come from sand, metal, or minerals. The organic matter stores energy that becomes usable once it is compressed and concentrated.

Blank Page

Science Assessment One—Correlation Chart

The Correlation Charts can be used by the teachers to identify areas of improvement. When students miss a question, place an "X" in the corresponding box. A column with a large number of "Xs" shows more practice is needed with that particular standard.

Correlation	SC.A.1.3.1	SC.A.1.3.3	SC.A.1.3.4	SC.A.1.3.5	SC.A.2.3.2	SC.B.1.3.1	SC.B.1.3.5	SC.B.1.3.5	SC.B.1.3.6	SC.B.2.3.1	SC.C.1.3.1	SC.C.2.3.1	SC.C.2.3.4	SC.C.2.3.6	SC.C.2.3.7	SC.D.1.3.1	SC.D.1.3.3	SC.D.1.3.4	SC.D.1.3.5	SC.E.1.3.4
Answer	**	D	H	B	H	**	D	F	C	H	C	I	D	**	G	D	G	A	H	B
Question	1	2	3	4	5	6	7	8	9	10	11	12	13	14	15	16	17	18	19	20

Student Names

*Gridded-Response Item/**Short-Response Item/***Extended-Response Item

Science Assessment One—Correlation Chart

Correlation	SC.E.1.3.4	SC.E.2.3.1	SC.F.1.3.1	SC.F.1.3.2	SC.F.1.3.3	SC.F.1.3.5	SC.F.1.3.6	SC.F.2.3.2	SC.G.1.3.3	SC.G.1.3.4	SC.G.2.3.1	SC.G.2.3.2	SC.G.2.3.3	SC.G.2.3.4	SC.H.1.3.1	SC.H.1.3.2	SC.H.1.3.1	SC.H.1.3.4	SC.H.3.3.1
Answer	H	D	H	D	F	A	I	A	F	A	F	D	H	A	F	C	G	***	B	F
Question	21	22	23	24	25	26	27	28	29	30	31	32	33	34	35	36	37	38	39	40

Student Names

*Gridded-Response Item/**Short-Response Item/***Extended-Response Item

Science Assessment One—Correlation Chart

Correlation	SC.A.1.3.2	SC.A.1.3.3	SC.A.2.3.2	SC.A.1.3.5	SC.B.1.3.6	SC.B.1.3.3	SC.A.1.3.6	SC.B.1.3.4	SC.B.1.3.3	SC.B.2.3.2
Answer	B	I	A	I	D	**	H	D	G	C
Question	41	42	43	44	45	46	47	48	49	50

Student Names

*Gridded-Response Item/**Short-Response Item/***Extended-Response Item

Science
Assessment Two

Science Assessment Two

Directions for Taking the Science Assessment Two

On this section of the Florida Comprehensive Assessment Test (FCAT), you will answer 50 questions.

For multiple-choice questions, you will be asked to pick the best answer out of four possible choices and fill in the answer in the answer bubble. On gridded-response questions, you will also fill in your answer in answer bubbles, but you will fill in numbers and symbols corresponding to the solution you obtain for a question. Fill in the answer bubbles and gridded-response answer bubbles on the Answer Sheets on pages 235–244 to mark your selection.

For "Read, Inquire, Explain" questions (short- and extended-response items) you will put your answers on the Answer Sheets, but be sure to show your work on your Answer Sheet because you will be scored on your work as well as on your answer.

Read each question carefully and answer it to the best of your ability. If you do not know an answer, you may skip the question and come back to it later.

Figures and diagrams with given lengths and/or dimensions are not drawn to scale. Angle measures should be assumed to be accurate. Use the Science Reference Sheet on page 37 and the Periodic Table on page 38 to help you answer the questions.

When you finish, check your answers.

1 Maria is on a train traveling 240 km from Station A to Station B along the route shown. If the train leaves Station A at 5:00 pm and arrives at Station B at 6:30 pm without stopping, what was its average speed in kilometers/hour?

STATION A

STATION B

240 MILES

2 READ INQUIRE EXPLAIN   Go to your Science Assessment Two Answer Sheet to answer Number 2.

 Go On

3 How does energy from an earthquake move from the point of origin?

    A. outward as waves
    B. inward as waves
    C. outward in a hollow beam
    D. inward in a hollow beam

4 Which of the following statements is **true** about energy?

    F. Energy can be created.
    G. Energy can be destroyed.
    H. Energy can be created or destroyed.
    I. Energy cannot be created or destroyed.

5 What will happen to an object that is in motion, such as the football shown below, if no force acts on it?

    A. It will slow down and then stop.
    B. It will stay in constant motion.
    C. It will speed up to terminal velocity.
    D. It will stop.

6 What type of force created the valley shown below?

F. plate movement
G. volcanic activity
H. erosion
I. deposition

7 Farmers sometimes say that you can tell good soil because it has a lot of earthworms in it. How do earthworms contribute to making soil good for plants?

A. They eat the bugs that would destroy plant roots.
B. They eat organic material and add nutrients to the soil.
C. They eat the seeds of weeds so that they do not take up soil space.
D. They eat plant roots so that they do not grow too deeply.

Copying is Prohibited

8 Which of the following organisms causes the decay of dead organisms?

F.

G.

H.

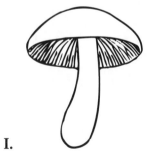

I.

Go On ▶

9 Which of the following landscapes will likely be **least** resistant to erosion?

A.

Forest

B.

Desert

C.

Grassland

D.

Swamp

10 Which of the following processes would typically take the **longest** amount of time to complete?

    F. a mountain is formed from plate movements
    G. an earthquake destroys several large buildings
    H. a new forest full of trees grows from seedlings following a forest fire
    I. constant action from waves wears away a beach

11 What forces are most likely responsible for creating the stone structures below?

    A. volcanoes
    B. water
    C. glaciers
    D. wind

12 Which of the following objects in our solar system is also a star?

    F. Saturn
    G. Halley's comet
    H. the Sun
    I. the Moon

13 Power plants often burn coal to make electricity for use by humans. What is one negative consequence of burning fossil fuels such as oil or coal for energy?

    A. It creates extra energy for use by society.
    B. It releases carbon dioxide into the atmosphere.
    C. It reduces the area in rainforests for wildlife.
    D. It increases the amount of usable oxygen in the air.

14 An Angstrom unit is used as which type of measurement?

    F. the distance between cities in a country
    G. the distance between the floor and surface of the ocean
    H. the distance between stars in the galaxy
    I. the distance between atoms

15 What does the image below show?

    A. a planet and moon system
    B. the solar system
    C. a galaxy
    D. the universe

16 Which of the following planets is made up of gas?

F. Mercury
G. Venus
H. Saturn
I. Mars

17 What do Mercury and Earth have in common?

A. They are made of the same type of material.
B. They are the same size.
C. They are the same distance from the Sun.
D. They have the same number of moons.

18 Which two materials are stars made of?

F. carbon and oxygen
G. hydrogen and oxygen
H. helium and hydrogen
I. carbon and helium

19 Which of the following is typically the same of any two stars?

A. their ages
B. their temperatures
C. their sizes
D. their compositions

20 How is the galaxy shown below probably **not** similar to our own Milky Way galaxy?

F. It is the same shape.
G. It is held together by gravity.
H. It is made of the same materials.
I. It contains the same forms of energy.

21 Go to your Science Assessment Two Answer Sheet to answer Number 21.

22 What is the smallest living part that makes up the organisms shown below?

rabbit   mushroom   plant

A. an atom
B. a cell
C. a tissue
D. an organ

23 Which of the following organisms is unicellular?

F. a human
G. a plant
H. a fungi
I. a bacterium

24 How does a multicellular organism form and repair organs and tissues as it grows?

A. The cells grow and divide.
B. The cells grow but do not divide.
C. The cells divide but do not grow.
D. The cells only accumulate in areas.

25 Which of the following describes the levels of organization in living organisms from simplest to most complex?

    F. tissues, cells, organs, organ systems
    G. organ systems, organs, tissues, cells
    H. cells, tissues, organs, organ systems
    I. organs, organ systems, cells, tissues

26 How do the different organs and tissues shown below act differently and do different jobs?

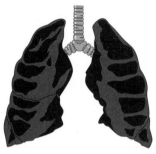

Lungs   Muscle Tissue

    A. The cells are organized differently.
    B. The cells are different types and structures.
    C. The tissues use different nutrients and energy sources.
    D. The tissues constantly change to do different tasks.

27 What can you most likely conclude about the cells that make up an organism that is sick or having health problems?

    F. You cannot tell anything about the cells.
    G. The cells are growing and dividing.
    H. The cells taking in more nutrients than normal.
    I. The cells are not functioning properly.

28 Many birds fly south for the winter each year. An organism's behavior is shaped by reactions to what type of changes?

    A. changes in other populations
    B. changes in the environment
    C. changes in kinetic energy
    D. changes in physical appearance

29 The yeast below is reproducing asexually.

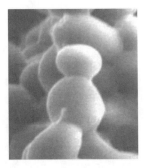

What is one advantage in reproducing asexually?

    F. It creates more diversity
    G. It causes new characteristics
    H. It requires only one parent
    I. It can result in new species

30 Go to your Science Assessment Two Answer Sheet to answer Number 30.

31 Which of the following provides evidence that organisms change over time?

    A. the fossil record
    B. the appearance of parents and offspring
    C. the behavior of an organism
    D. a DNA sample

32 Which of the following characteristics would best help an organism survive and reproduce in a desert environment?

    F. the ability to see in the dark
    G. an extra layer of thick fur
    H. skin that traps and holds in water
    I. feet with long sharp claws

33 Why do some scientists not consider a virus to be a living organism?

    A. A virus does not have DNA or RNA.
    B. A virus cannot reproduce.
    C. A virus needs another organism to replicate.
    D. A virus cannot obtain energy to survive.

34 The flow of what is represented by the arrows in this food web?

     F. water
     G. housing
     H. reproduction
     I. energy

35 Which of the following resources is non-renewable?

     A. coal
     B. water
     C. air
     D. soil

36 The graph below shows the cumulative loss of forest area, as well as an estimate of continued future losses.

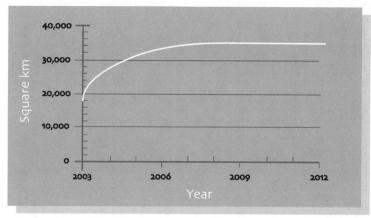

Cumulative Loss of Forest Area

How many more square kilometers of forest area were lost between the years 2003 and 2004?

37 When two similar studies yield different conclusions, which of the following would **not** be a way of determining which conclusion is more accurate?

F. Conduct another experiment to examine the same issue.
G. Examine the details of both experiments' methods.
H. Reevaluate both experiments' data.
I. Determine which conclusion appears to make the most sense to the most number of scientists.

38 Why is it important to share and communicate the processes of a scientific investigation as well as the results?

A. It allows the results to be changed if they don't agree with the hypothesis.
B. It allows other scientists to examine the procedure and verify the results.
C. It allows other scientists to copy the procedure and take the credit.
D. It allows the procedure to be changed if the results do not agree with the theory.

39 Go to your Science Assessment Two Answer Sheet to answer Number 39.

40 The frequency of a wavelength can be calculated by the equation: frequency = speed/wavelength. If you use meters and seconds as your units, the frequency answer will be in units of hertz (Hz). If the speed of the wavelength shown below is 325 meters/second, calculate the frequency in **hertz**.

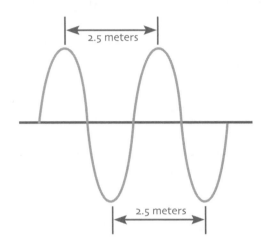

2.5 meters

2.5 meters

41 We eat food to get energy to live. Where does the energy for all food ultimately come from?

    F. the ocean
    G. the air
    H. the Sun
    I. the Moon

 42 READ INQUIRE EXPLAIN Go to your Science Assessment Two Answer Sheet to answer Number 42.

Go On

43 A scientist measured how adding weight to a race car affected its speed. The results of the investigation are shown in the table below.

Weight added (kg)	Speed (km/hr)
10	125
20	120
30	115

What would you predict the speed of the car to be if the scientist added 50 kg of weight to the car?

44 The population of bacteria in a dental study is shown on the graph below.

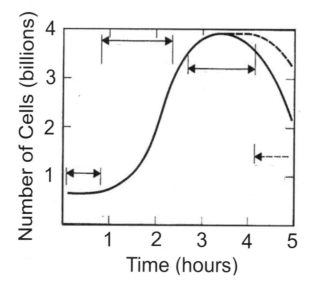

What can you determine about the growth of the bacteria from this data?

A. It increases with time.
B. It decreases with time.
C. It increases, then decreases with time.
D. It decreases, then increases with time.

45 Go to your Science Assessment Two Answer Sheet to answer Number 45.

46 Once a scientist has conducted an investigation, collected data, and reached a conclusion, what important step must still be done in order to make sure the knowledge contributes to science?

    F. The scientist should make the information available to everyone.
    G. The scientist should make adjustments to the data so that it is easy to understand.
    H. The scientist should keep the information secret while they do more work.
    I. The scientist should keep changing the data until it agrees with the hypothesis.

47 Which of the following things do all scientific disciplines use to find answers?

    A. microscopes
    B. computers
    C. measuring tools
    D. scientific methods

48 Shellie and Mark are testing different fertilizers to see which make tomatoes grow bigger. Shellie's experiment shows that fertilizer A makes bigger tomatoes, but Mark's experiment shows that fertilizer B makes bigger tomatoes. How should Shellie and Mark decide which data and investigation is valid?

F. They vote on the results of the investigation.
G. They should repeat the investigation.
H. They make sure that no one objects to the data.
I. They should do an opposite investigation.

49 The distance of each planet from the Sun is measured in Astronomical Units, or AUs. The distances of the planets in our solar system are given below in AUs.

Mercury	.39
Venus	.72
Earth	1.0
Mars	1.52
Jupiter	5.2
Saturn	9.54
Uranus	19.18
Neptune	30.06
Pluto	39.52

If one astronomical unit is approximately 93,000,000 miles, approximately how many million miles away from the sun is the planet Jupiter?

50 The Human Genome Project is a group of scientists from many nations who worked together to map out the genetic sequences in human DNA. As this group of scientists mapped the genome, they published their results for everyone to see and use. Why did they do this?

A. It is international law that all scientific results must be revealed.
B. They revealed the information in order to claim ownership of it.
C. By revealing the information, they enabled others to do research with it.
D. They revealed the information in order to discredit other scientists.

This is the end of the Science Assessment Two.
Until time is called, go back and check your work or answer
questions you did not complete. When you have finished, close
your workbook.

Answer Sheet

Name_____

Science Assessment Two Answer Sheet

Answer all the questions that appear in Science Assessment Two on this Answer Sheet.
Answer multiple-choice questions by filling in the bubble for the answer you select.
Answer gridded-response questions by filling in the correct bubbles. Write your
answers to "Read, Inquire, Explain" questions on the lines provided.

To remove your Answer Sheet, carefully tear along the dotted line.

Fold and Tear Carefully Along Dotted Line.

Fold and Tear Carefully Along Dotted Line.

2 A cart is rolling eastward.

Part A Describe how the motion of the cart would be affected by an additional eastward force.

_____

_____

_____

_____

_____

Part B Explain how the motion of the cart would change in each condition described.

    1. A westward force that is equal to the original eastward force is applied to the cart.

_____

_____

    2. A westward force that is greater than the original eastward force is applied to the cart.

_____

_____

    3. A westward force that is less than the original eastward force is applied to the cart.

_____

_____

Go On

3 Ⓐ Ⓑ Ⓒ Ⓓ

4 Ⓕ Ⓖ Ⓗ Ⓘ

5 Ⓐ Ⓑ Ⓒ Ⓓ

6 Ⓕ Ⓖ Ⓗ Ⓘ

7 Ⓐ Ⓑ Ⓒ Ⓓ

8 Ⓕ Ⓖ Ⓗ Ⓘ

9 Ⓐ Ⓑ Ⓒ Ⓓ

10 Ⓕ Ⓖ Ⓗ Ⓘ

11 Ⓐ Ⓑ Ⓒ Ⓓ

12 Ⓕ Ⓖ Ⓗ Ⓘ

13 Ⓐ Ⓑ Ⓒ Ⓓ

14 Ⓕ Ⓖ Ⓗ Ⓘ

15 Ⓐ Ⓑ Ⓒ Ⓓ

16 Ⓕ Ⓖ Ⓗ Ⓘ

17 Ⓐ Ⓑ Ⓒ Ⓓ

18 Ⓕ Ⓖ Ⓗ Ⓘ

19 Ⓐ Ⓑ Ⓒ Ⓓ

20 Ⓕ Ⓖ Ⓗ Ⓘ

Fold and Tear Carefully Along Dotted Line.

Go On ▶

21 Describe how the body system below works to help humans live.

_____

_____

_____

_____

_____

22 Ⓐ Ⓑ Ⓒ Ⓓ   **23** Ⓕ Ⓖ Ⓗ Ⓘ   **24** Ⓐ Ⓑ Ⓒ Ⓓ

25 Ⓕ Ⓖ Ⓗ Ⓘ   **26** Ⓐ Ⓑ Ⓒ Ⓓ   **27** Ⓕ Ⓖ Ⓗ Ⓘ

28 Ⓐ Ⓑ Ⓒ Ⓓ   **29** Ⓕ Ⓖ Ⓗ Ⓘ

Go On ▶

30 Why do different offspring of the same two parents exhibit different characteristics?

READ
INQUIRE
EXPLAIN

_____

_____

_____

_____

_____

31 Ⓐ Ⓑ Ⓒ Ⓓ   **32** Ⓕ Ⓖ Ⓗ Ⓘ   **33** Ⓐ Ⓑ Ⓒ Ⓓ

34 Ⓕ Ⓖ Ⓗ Ⓘ   **35** Ⓐ Ⓑ Ⓒ Ⓓ   **36**

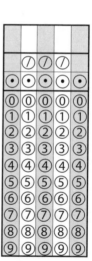

Fold and Tear Carefully Along Dotted Line.

37 Ⓕ Ⓖ Ⓗ Ⓘ   **38** Ⓐ Ⓑ Ⓒ Ⓓ

39 Why is it important for a scientist to keep accurate and honest records while performing an investigation?

READ
INQUIRE
EXPLAIN

_____

_____

_____

_____

_____

40

41 Ⓕ Ⓖ Ⓗ Ⓘ

Fold and Tear Carefully Along Dotted Line.

42 Almost all scientists use computers to help them with research.

READ
INQUIRE
EXPLAIN

Describe how using a computer can make science easier and faster.

_____

_____

_____

_____

_____

_____

_____

_____

_____

43

44 Ⓐ Ⓑ Ⓒ Ⓓ

Fold and Tear Carefully Along Dotted Line.

Copying is Prohibited
© Englefield & Associates, Inc.

45 You are working as a scientist to test a new medicine. You will need to use people who are sick and have them try the medicine to see how well it works.

READ
INQUIRE
EXPLAIN

Part A What sorts of things should you consider when using humans in research?

_____

_____

_____

_____

_____

Part B What types of things will you need to tell the people who are in your experiment?

_____

_____

_____

_____

_____

Go On

46 Ⓕ Ⓖ Ⓗ Ⓘ

47 Ⓐ Ⓑ Ⓒ Ⓓ

48 Ⓕ Ⓖ Ⓗ Ⓘ

49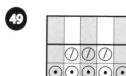

50 Ⓐ Ⓑ Ⓒ Ⓓ

Fold and Tear Carefully Along Dotted Line.

Go On ▶

This is the end of the Science Assessment Two—Answer Sheet.
Until time is called, go back and check your work or answer questions you did not complete. When you have finished, close your workbook.

Science Assessment Two: Skills Chart

Question	Standard	Answer	Keywords
1	SC.C.1.3.1	160	Motion can be described by position, direction, and speed
2	SC.C.2.3.6	see analysis	Net force can act on an object
3	SC.C.1.3.2	A	The difference between weight and mass
4	SC.B.1.3.2	I	Energy cannot be created or destroyed only changed from one form to another
5	SC.C.2.3.5	B	Net force can act on an object
6	SC.D.1.3.1	H	Mechanical and chemical activities shape and reshape Earth's surface
7	SC.D.1.3.4	B	Ways in which plants and animals reshape the landscape
8	SC.D.1.3.4	I	Ways in which plants and animals reshape the landscape
9	SC.D.1.3.4	B	Ways in which plants and animals reshape the landscape
10	SC.D.1.3.5	F	Concepts of time and size relating to the interaction of Earth's processes
11	SC.D.1.3.1	D	Mechanical and chemical activities shape and reshape Earth's surface
12	SC.E.1.3.3	H	The Sun is one of the many stars in our galaxy
13	SC.D.2.3.2	B	Positive and Negative consequences of human action on the Earth's system
14	SC.D.1.3.5	I	Concepts of time and size relating to the interaction of Earth's processes
15	SC.E.1.3.1	B	Vast size of our Solar System
16	SC.E.1.3.1	H	Vast size of our Solar System
17	SC.E.1.3.1	A	Vast size of our Solar System
18	SC.E.1.3.4	H	Stars appear to be made of similar elements
19	SC.E.1.3.4	D	Stars appear to be made of similar elements
20	SC.E.2.3.1	F	Other galaxies appear similar in element, forces, and energy found in our Solar System
21	SC.F.1.3.1	see analysis	Living things are composed of systems that function in reproduction, growth, maintenance, and regulation
22	SC.F.1.3.2	B	Organisms that are single-celled and multicellular
23	SC.F.1.3.2	I	Organisms that are single-celled and multicellular
24	SC.F.1.3.3	A	Multicellular organisms
25	SC.F.1.3.4	H	Structural organization of living things

Science Assessment Two: Skills Chart

Question	Standard	Answer	Keywords
26	SC.F.1.3.6	B	Functions of cells
27	SC.F.1.3.5	I	Life functions of organisms are related to what occurs with the cell
28	SC.F.1.3.7	B	Behavior is a response to environment and influences growth and development
29	SC.F.2.3.1	H	The patterns and advantages of sexual and asexual reproduction in plants and animals
30	SC.F.2.3.2	see analysis	Variation in species due to genetic information passed from parent to offspring
31	SC.F.2.3.4	A	Fossil records provide evidence of changes over time
32	SC.F.2.3.3	I	Organisms live long enough to reproduce because they have survival characteristics
33	SC.G.1.3.1	C	Viruses depend on other living things
34	SC.G.1.3.4	I	Interactions resulting in the flow of energy and the cycling of matter throughout a system
35	SC.G.2.3.1	A	Renewable and nonrenewable resources
36	SC.G.2.3.4	8,000-10,000	Humans are part of an ecosystem and their activities may alter the equilibrium in ecosystems
37	SC.H.1.3.1	I	New information challenges prevailing theories
38	SC.H.1.3.2	B	Study of events that led scientists to discoveries can provide information about the process and effects
39	SC.H.1.3.4	see analysis	Accurate record keeping, openness, and replication are essential to credibility
40	SC.B.1.3.6	130	Properties of waves
41	SC.G.1.3.5	H	Life is maintained by input of energy from the Sun and by the recycling of atoms
42	SC.H.3.3.7	see analysis	Computers speed up collection and analysis
43	SC.H.1.3.5	105	Change in one or more variables may alter outcome of an investigation
44	SC.H.2.3.1	C	Patterns exist within and across systems
45	SC.H.3.3.1	see analysis	Science ethics
46	SC.H.3.3.6	F	Knowledge and technology can eventually become available to everyone
47	SC.H.1.3.3	D	Science discipline share a common purpose, philosophy, enterprise
48	SC.H.1.3.7	G	Similar investigations give different results
49	SC.D.1.3.5	483.6	Concepts of time and size relating to the interaction of Earth's processes
50	SC.H.3.3.4	C	Ethical and aesthtic values

Science Assessment Two—Answer Key

1 Maria is on a train traveling 240 km from Station A to Station B along the route shown. If the train leaves Station A at 5:00 pm and arrives at Station B at 6:30 pm without stopping, what was its average speed in kilometers/hour?

What is the average speed of Maria's train in kilometers/hour?
Analysis: *The correct answer is 160 km/hour. 240 kilometers/1.5 hours = 160 kilometers/hour.*

2 A cart is rolling eastward.

Part A Describe how the motion of the cart would be affected by an additional eastward force.
Part B Explain how the motion of the cart would change in each condition described.
1. A westward force that is equal to the original eastward force is applied to the cart.
2. A westward force that is greater than the original eastward force is applied to the cart.
3. A westward force that is less than the original eastward force is applied to the cart.
Analysis: *Extended-response answers may vary.* **Part A** Answers should reflect the fact that an eastward force (in the same direction as the cart is moving) will increase the speed of the cart. **Part B 1.** The westward force will act against the force of the cart and either slow it down if the force is less. **2.** The westward force will stop the cart if the force is equal. **3.** The westward force will move the cart in the opposite direction if the force is greater.

3 How does energy from an earthquake move from the point of origin?
Analysis: *Choice A is correct.* Energy from an earthquake moves outward from the point of origin as waves. Energy that moves this way often creates visible ripples or damage as it moves. Energy does not move inward or in beams.

4 Which of the following statements is **true** about energy?
Analysis: *Choice I is correct.* Energy cannot be created or destroyed. It can only be transformed. When energy seems to disappear or appear it is only because it is transforming into a different form of energy or matter.

5 What will happen to an object that is in motion, such as the football shown below, if no force acts on it?

Analysis: *Choice B is correct.* An object in motion will stay in motion until a force acts on it. Similarly, an object at rest will stay at rest until a force acts on it. Most objects in motion will eventually slow down and stop because of the force of friction acting on it.

6 What type of force created the valley shown below?

Analysis: *Choice H is correct.* Valleys, such as the one shown, are created as rivers run through and constantly erode the land. After a long period of time the river cuts deeper and deeper until a valley is created. Other forces, such as volcanoes and deposition, can create other types of landforms such as mountains or deltas.

7 Farmers sometimes say that you can tell good soil because it has a lot of earthworms in it. How do earthworms contribute to making soil good for plants?
Analysis: *Choice B is correct.* Worms and other organisms such as fungi, bacteria, and insects help recycle nutrients by decomposing organic material in the soil. The earthworms eat plant and animal materials and break them down into nitrogen and carbon nutrients that are used by plants.

Science Assessment Two—Answer Key

8 Which of the following organisms causes the decay of dead organisms?

Analysis: *Choice I is correct.*
Fungi are decomposers. They break down plant and animal material into basic components that plants are able to use. Spiders and eagles are heterotrophs that eat other organisms for energy. Trees are autotrophs that make energy from sunlight.

9 Which of the following landscapes will likely be **least** resistant to erosion?

Analysis: *Choice B is correct.*
Soil is susceptible to erosion when it does not have plants growing in it. Plant roots sink into the soil and hold it together so that it is not washed away by rain and water. Forests, swamps, and grasslands all have an abundance of plants that hold the soil in place.

10 Which of the following processes would typically take the **longest** amount of time to complete?
Analysis: *Choice F is correct.*
Mountains take millions of years to form as plates shift and move crust and magma upward. Other processes, such as the formation of a forest or erosion of a beach can occur in tens or hundreds of years. Earthquakes can destroy areas in a matter of minutes.

11 What forces are most likely responsible for creating the stone structures below?

Analysis: *Choice D is correct.* Wind shapes Earth's surface by moving sediment and eroding rock and soil. The structures shown have been eroded by wind. Some areas of rock are harder than other areas. As wind constantly blows, it erodes the softer rock and leaves the harder rock to make various forms. Volcanoes can shape the surface by creating mountains or spewing magma and lava. Water can cause erosion of rocks as well; however this is a desert environment with little to no running water that could cause erosion. Glaciers can flatten land or leave sediments as they retreat.

Science Assessment Two—Answer Key

12 Which of the following objects in our solar system is also a star?
Analysis: *Choice H is correct.* The Sun in our solar system is also a star. All stars have similar makeup, although they can be different sizes, colors, and distances. Saturn, comets, and moons are very dissimilar to stars, since they are made of rock or gas and do not emit energy like stars do.

13 Power plants often burn coal to make electricity for use by humans. What is one negative consequence of burning fossil fuels such as oil or coal for energy?
Analysis: *Choice B is correct.* Humans can affect the environment in positive and negative ways. Although burning fossil fuels provides us with usable energy is a positive effect, it also releases carbon dioxide into the atmosphere as a negative impact. This carbon dioxide may be responsible for increasing global temperatures. Burning fossil fuels does not pollute the oceans or release oxygen.

14 An angstrom unit is used as which type of measurement?
Analysis: *Choice I is correct.* An angstrom is used to measure the distance between atoms. Astronomical units, or AUs, are used to measure the distances between stars. Distances between countries can be measured in kilometers and distances in the ocean are measured as fathoms.

15 What does the image below show?

Analysis: *Choice B is correct.* The solar system is made up of the Sun and all the planets and moons that orbit it. A planet and moon system is made up of one planet with one or several moons orbiting it. A galaxy, such as the Milky Way galaxy is a collection of millions of stars. The universe consists of everything in space.

16 Which of the following planets is made up of gas?
Analysis: *Choice H is correct.* The outer planets, including Saturn, are known as gas giants because they are made up of gas. The inner planets, such as Mercury, Venus, Earth, and Mars, are made of rock.

17 What do Mercury and Earth have in common?
Analysis: *Choice A is correct.* Earth and Mercury are different sizes, are different distances from the Sun, and have different amounts of moons. They are both inner planets that are made of rock.

18 Which two materials are stars made of?
Analysis: *Choice H is correct.* Stars are made of hydrogen and helium gases. The hydrogen gas releases energy as fusion occurs and creates helium.

19 Which of the following is typically the same of any two stars?
Analysis: *Choice D is correct.* Although stars can vary in age, temperatures, sizes, colors, and distances, all stars are made of basically the same chemical elements: hydrogen and helium.

20 How is the galaxy show below probably **not** similar to our own Milky Way galaxy?

Analysis: *Choice F is correct.* Galaxies all contain stars and systems held together by gravity. They are all made up of the same materials with the same forms of energy. However, galaxies vary in their shapes. The Milky Way galaxy is disk-shaped with spiral arms, while the galaxy shown in the picture is elliptical.

Science Assessment Two—Answer Key

21 Describe how the body system below works to help humans live?

Analysis: *Short-response answers may vary.* The system shown in the illustration is the circulatory system. This system uses blood to move things around the body. The circulatory system transports oxygen and nutrients to the cells and body organs that need them and picks up carbon dioxide and other wastes from the cells and removes them from the body.

22 What is the smallest living part that makes up the organisms shown below?

rabbit   mushroom   plant

Analysis: *Choice B is correct.* The cell is the smallest living part of most organisms, including multicellular organisms such as plants, rabbits, and birds. Although an atom is smaller, it is not living and atoms make up everything, including nonliving things. Both tissues and organs are made up of cells.

23 Which of the following organisms is unicellular?
Analysis: *Choice I is correct.* A Bacterium is a single-celled organism. Humans and plants are multi-cellular organisms. Although some fungi, called yeasts, can be single-celled, most fungi are multi-cellular organisms.

24 How does a multicellular organism form and repair organs and tissues as it grows?
Analysis: *Choice A is correct.* As organisms grow, they produce more cells. These cells then become larger and often take on different characteristics in order to do special jobs.

25 Which of the following describes the levels of organization in living organisms from simplest to the most complex?
Analysis: *Choice H is correct.* The basic component of living things are cells. Groups of similar cells combine to make tissues. Tissues work together to make up organs, and organs work as a system to do specific tasks.

26 How do the different organs and tissues show below act differently and do different jobs?

Lungs   **Muscle Tissue**

Analysis: *Choice B is correct.* The heart and other specialized organs are made up of cells and tissues that are different types and structures. The cells that make up the heart are different from the cells that make up bone or brain tissue. The different structures help the cells do different jobs.

27 What can you most likely conclude about the cells that make up an organism that is sick or having health problems?
Analysis: *Choice I is correct.* The function of an organism's cells determines the functioning of the organism. When there are problems on the cellular level, the organism suffers as well.

28 Many birds fly south for the winter each year. An organism's behavior is shaped by reactions to what type of changes?
Analysis: *Choice B is correct.* Organisms react to their environment. Changes in the environment mean that an organism must react to adapt or else it may fail to survive. Changes in other populations, kinetic energy, or physical appearances do not directly influence behavior.

29 The yeast below is reproducing asexually.

What is one advantage to reproducing asexually?
Analysis: *Choice H is correct.* Sexual reproduction adds more diversity and creates new characteristics and sometimes new species. The advantage to reproducing asexually is that only one parent is required.

Science Assessment Two—Answer Key

30 Why do offspring that result from sexual reproduction often have different mixtures of characteristics from both parents?
Analysis: Short-response answers may vary. The traits and characteristics that children have are coded by the genetic material that they inherit from their parents. Because children get exactly half of their genetic material from each parent, they typically also get a mixture of traits from the two parents. Since the mixture of genetic material is random, the traits that they get are somewhat random, meaning that children will usually each have different random combinations of traits from each parent.

31 Which of the following provides evidence that organisms change over time?
Analysis: *Choice A is correct.* Changes that happen to organisms over time take many generations. The fossil record shows the preserved remains of organisms over millions of years. Parents and offspring show only small changes between individuals. Behavior does not indicate change over time since only recent organisms can be studied. DNA samples can show the genes that give an organism its characteristics, but you must have samples from organisms for thousands of years to chart changes over time.

32 Which of the following characteristics would best help an organism survive and reproduce in a desert environment?

Analysis: *Choice H is correct.* Organisms develop characteristics that help them survive and reproduce in specific environments. An organism that must thrive in the desert typically has characteristics that deal with the intense sun and lack of water. An organism with skin that holds in water can help the organism survive by preventing drying out. Characteristics such as thick fur, the ability to see in the dark, and sharp claws are not specially suited for the desert environment.

33 Why do some scientists not consider a virus to be a living organism?
Analysis: *Choice C is correct.* Viruses have DNA or RNA, utilize energy to survive, and reproduce. But a virus needs a host organism in order to reproduce itself. Viruses are lifeless without the host.

34 The flow of what is represented by the arrows in this food web?

Analysis: *Choice I is correct.* A food web shows how energy moves through a community of organisms in an environment. The arrows show the direction that energy moves as organisms eat food. Food webs do not show the movement of water, reproduction, or housing.

35 Which of the following resources is nonrenewable?
Analysis: *Choice A is correct.* Coal is a non-renewable resource because, as it is used, it is not replaced in nature-at least on a human time scale. Air, wind, and water are all renewable resources because as long as they are managed properly, they can last indefinitely.

Science Assessment Two—Answer Key

36 The graph below shows the cumulative loss of forest area, as well as an estimate of continued near future losses.

Cumulative Loss of Forest Area

How many more square kilometers of forest area were lost between 2003 and 2004?

Analysis: In 2003, according to the graph, 18,000 square kilometers of forest area had been lost. By 2004, somewhere between 26,000 and 28,000 square kilometers were lost. The difference is 8,000 to 10,000 square kilometers.

37 When two similar studies yield different conclusions, which of the following would **not** be a way of determining which conclusion is more accurate?

Analysis: *Choice I is correct.* It suggests a process based on opinion, not on evaluation of data and observation. Choice F is incorrect because further experimentation is a common way to support past conclusions. Choices G and H are incorrect because determining if one experiment has flawed procedures or data evaluation is one way to choose between conclusions.

38 Why is it important to share and communicate the processes of a scientific investigation as well as the results?

Analysis: *Choice B is correct.* All scientists must publish the results and procedures they use in scientific investigation so that other scientists may examine them. A valid investigation should be able to be repeated by other scientists and allow them to get the same results.

39 Why is it important for a scientist to keep accurate and honest records while performing an investigation?

Analysis: *Short-response answers may vary.* Scientists must make efforts to keep complete and honest records of their investigations. Science depends on the honest efforts of scientists to remain objective and open their experiments to criticism. Only when records can be verified and when results are repeatable by others will the results of an experiment be valued as scientific information.

40 The frequency of a wavelength can be calculated by the equation: frequency = speed / wavelength. If you use meters and seconds as your units, the frequency answer will be in units of hertz (Hz). If the speed of the wavelength shown below is 325 meters / second, calculate the frequency in **hertz**.

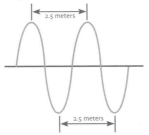

2.5 meters

2.5 meters

Analysis:
frequency = speed / wavelength
frequency = 325 meters / 2.5 meters
frequency = 130 hZ.

41 We eat food to get energy to live. Where does the energy for all food ultimately come from?

Analysis: *Choice H is correct.* The energy that goes into the food we eat comes from the Sun. The Sun sends light energy to Earth that is captured by plants during photosynthesis. Photosynthesis transforms the light energy into chemical energy that is stored in the plant and then eaten by humans.

42 Almost all scientists use computers to help them with research. Describe how using a computer can make science easier and faster.

Analysis: *Extended-response answers may vary.* The answer can include a variety of examples. Computers can help analyze data by performing complex calculations quickly. Data can also be sorted and displayed in a variety of ways that communicate results. Using computers helps scientists work with information quickly and communicate results effectively.

43 A scientist measured how adding weight to a race car affected its speed. The results of the investigation are shown in the table below.

Weight added (kg)	Speed (km/hr)
10	125
20	120
30	115

What would you predict the speed of the car to be if the scientist added 50 kg of weight to the car?

Analysis: *The correct answer is 105 km/hour.* With each additional 10 kg added to the weight of the car, the speed decreases by 5 km. Following this pattern, if the car weighs 50 kg, the speed will be 105 km/hour.

Copying is Prohibited

Science Assessment Two—Answer Key

44 The population of bacteria in a dental study is shown on the graph below.

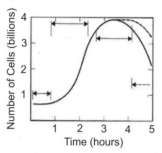

What can you determine about the growth of the bacteria from this data?
Analysis: *Choice C is correct.* The graph shows that the population of bacteria first increases, as shown by the upward movement of the line as it moves from left to right (as time passes). Then the population reaches a peak and begins to decline, as shown by the movement of the population line downward.

45 You are working as a scientist to test a new medicine. You will need to use people who are sick and have them try the medicine to see how well it works.
Part A What sorts of things should you consider when using humans in research?
Part B What types of things will you need to tell the people who are in your experiment?
Analysis: *Extended-response answers may vary.* Human research subjects should be aware of what participating in the study will mean. The researcher should inform the subjects of the risks that are involved. The participants should be able to weigh the risks against the possible benefits in order to make an informed choice about whether to participate or not. All possible safety precautions should be taken, and participants should be given the right to refuse to participate if they choose.

46 Once a scientist has conducted an investigation, collected data, and reached a conclusion, what important step must still be done in order to make sure the knowledge contributes to science?
Analysis: *Choice F is correct.* Scientific knowledge becomes helpful once it is available to everyone to use. Scientists publish their results so that other scientists can add to their work and people in other disciplines can use the information in different ways. Scientists should not keep information secret or tamper with data or results when communicating, since this only serves to hamper knowledge and progress.

47 Which of the following things do all scientific disciplines use to find answers?
Analysis: *Choice D is correct.* No matter which discipline or area of science is being explored, all scientists use scientific methods to discover information. These steps ensure that an investigation is carried out logically and gets the best information possible.

48 Shellie and Mark are testing different fertilizers to see which make tomatoes grow bigger. Shellie's experiment shows that fertilizer A makes bigger tomatoes, but Mark's experiment shows that fertilizer B makes bigger tomatoes. How should Shellie and Mark decide which data and investigation is valid?
Analysis: *Choice G is correct.* When scientific investigations give different results, it is important for the scientists to repeat the investigation as many times as possible. The investigations must be carried out using the same procedures and materials, being careful to duplicate things exactly.

49 The distance of each planet from the Sun is measured in Astronomical Units, or AUs. The distances of the planets in our solar system are given below in AUs.

Mercury	.39
Venus	.72
Earth	1.0
Mars	1.52
Jupiter	5.2
Saturn	9.54
Uranus	19.18
Neptune	30.06
Pluto	39.52

If one Astronomical unit is approximately 93,000,000 mile , approximately how many million miles away from the Sun is the planet Jupiter?
Analysis: *The correct answer is 483.6. (93 million miles x 5.2 AUs = 483.6 million miles)*

50 The Human Genome Project is a group of scientists from many nations who worked together to map out the genetic sequences in human DNA. As this group of scientists mapped the genome, they published their results for everyone to see and use. Why did they do this?
Analysis: *Choice C is correct.* An important part of doing scientific research is making the knowledge available to other scientists. When scientific knowledge is freely shared, it enables other scientists to check the work and do further research, sometimes in different fields or with varied purposes. The Human Genome Project released information so that scientists all over the world, working in many different applications, could use it to do further research.

Science Assessment Two—Correlation Chart

The Correlation Charts can be used by the teachers to identify areas of improvement. When students miss a question, place an "X" in the corresponding box. A column with a large number of "Xs" shows more practice is needed with that particular standard.

Correlation	SC.C.1.3.1	SC.C.2.3.6	SC.C.1.3.2	SC.B.1.3.2	SC.C.2.3.5	SC.D.1.3.1	SC.D.1.3.4	SC.D.1.3.4	SC.D.1.3.4	SC.D.1.3.5	SC.D.1.3.1	SC.E.1.3.3	SC.D.2.3.2	SC.D.1.3.5	SC.E.1.3.1	SC.E.1.3.1	SC.E.1.3.1	SC.D.1.3.4	SC.D.1.3.4	SC.E.2.3.1
Answer	*	***	A	I	B	H	B	I	B	F	D	H	B	I	B	H	A	H	D	F
Question	1	2	3	4	5	6	7	8	9	10	11	12	13	14	15	16	17	18	19	20

Student Names

*Gridded-Response Item/**Short-Response Item/***Extended-Response Item

Science Assessment Two—Correlation Chart

Correlation	SC.F.1.3.1	SC.F.1.3.2	SC.F.1.3.2	SC.F.1.3.3	SC.F.1.3.4	SC.F.1.3.6	SC.F.1.3.5	SC.F.1.3.7	SC.F.2.3.1	SC.F.2.3.2	SC.F.2.3.4	SC.F.2.3.3	SC.G.1.3.1	SC.G.1.3.4	SC.G.2.3.1	SC.G.2.3.4	SC.H.1.3.1	SC.H.1.3.2	SC.H.1.3.4	SC.B.1.3.6
Answer	**	B	I	A	H	B	I	B	H	**	A	H	C	I	A	*	I	B	**	*
Question	21	22	23	24	25	26	27	28	29	30	31	32	33	34	35	36	37	38	39	40

Student Names

*Gridded-Response Item/**Short-Response Item/***Extended-Response Item

Science Assessment Two—Correlation Chart

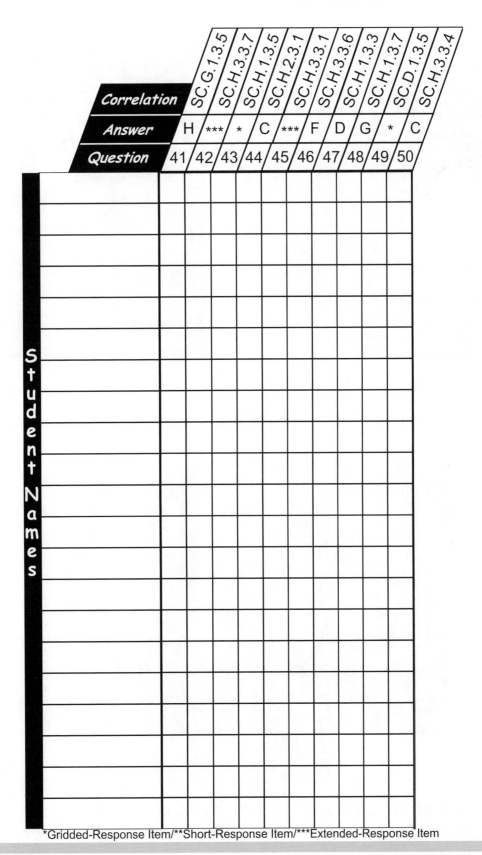

Correlation	SC.G.1.3.5	SC.H.3.3.7	SC.H.1.3.5	SC.H.2.3.1	SC.H.3.3.1	SC.H.3.3.6	SC.H.1.3.3	SC.H.1.3.7	SC.D.1.3.5	SC.H.3.3.4
Answer	H	***	*	C	***	F	D	G	*	C
Question	41	42	43	44	45	46	47	48	49	50

*Gridded-Response Item/**Short-Response Item/***Extended-Response Item

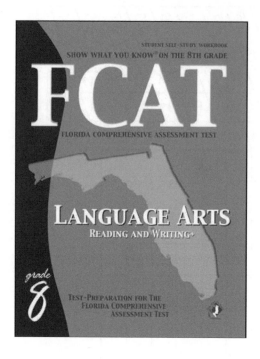
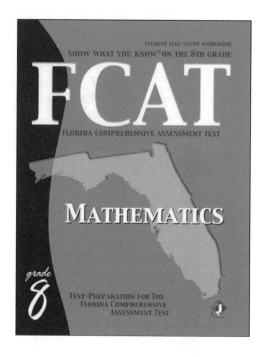